POSITIVE
Leadership

The Game Changer At Work

Steve Gladis, Ph.D.

Disclaimer

Part 1 is a summation of research about positivity and happiness, which I offer to inform, motivate, and inspire leaders. It is presented with the understanding that neither I nor the publisher is engaged in rendering any type of psychological, legal, or any other kind of professional advice.

Part 2 is a work of fiction. As such, all names, characters, places, and incidents are products of the author's imagination or are used fictionally. Any resemblance to actual persons (living or dead), businesses, organizations, events, or locales is entirely coincidental.

ISBN: 0-9891314-0-8
ISBN 13: 978-0-9891314-0-7
Library of Congress Control Number: 2013904908
Steve Gladis Leadership Partners, Annandale, VA

Dedication

This book is dedicated to Dean McIntyre, my best friend, a Renaissance man, and a technical genius. Without a doubt, Dean is the happiest and most positive person I've had the pleasure to know. No matter the problem, issue, or puzzle—Dean solves it without ever getting upset. He's the best example I know of a positive leader. The energy from his positivity could light a medium-sized city!

Acknowledgments

Donna Gladis, my wife, confidant, and most trusted friend. Dean McIntyre, my friend and technical advisor. Joanne Lozar Glenn, my trusted editor, and Mariann Baker, my eagle-eyed proofreader. Also, Martin Seligman, Sonja Lyubomerski , Barbara Frederickson, Ed Diener, Shawn Achor, Tal Ben-Shahar, Richard Boyatzis, Tom Rath, Daniel Goleman, and all those researching the areas of positive psychology and leadership. Beth Cabrera and Matthew Della Porta for reviewing the manuscript focused on the positivity research. My test readers: Kathy Albarado, Scott Sheafe, Janet Amirault, Rosemary Covey, Susan Wight, Jim Lockett, Lauren Semper Scott, and Debra and Brian Kabalkin.

Table of Contents

Introduction

I spent a year "researching the researchers" on positive psychology and applied that research to leadership, my life's obsession. I read the works of Martin Seligman, Ed Diener, Richard Boyatzis, Daniel Goleman, Tom Rath, Barbara Frederickson, Sonja Lyubomirsky, Shawn Achor, Tal Ben-Shahar, and others. All that "researching the researchers," and my personal experience as a leader in the U.S. Marine Corps, the FBI, and as an executive coach, have helped me discover what I call Positive Leadership: The Game Changer at Work. Positive Leadership (PL) literally morphs the workplace from a place where people work at a job to one where they thrive. Indeed, working on this book and practicing the techniques, you'll find throughout it, has made this the happiest, most positive year of my life. Ironically I'm actually a bit sad that it's over. However, I am buoyed by the fact that I get to give presentations on the book to business folks, who enjoy getting the information on Positive Leadership almost as much as I enjoy offering it.

Part I is written like an article you might read in *The Harvard Business Review* or *T+D Magazine* (*Training and Development*). It's straightforward and attempts to describe Positive Leadership and answer three big questions:

1. What is positivity?
2. Why is positivity so important for leaders?
3. How can leaders increase positivity?

Part II tells a story—it's a leadership fable, a fictionalized case study about how positivity and happiness work in "real life." For many years, I've been coaching and teaching leadership and communication to corporate and government clients. And while this story is a fable and the characters entirely fictional, it's a collage of circumstances and experiences that are close to life and demonstrate how positivity and happiness function to influence leadership. It's worth noting that the research on storytelling as an instructional and motivational tool is compelling (Gladis, 2008). Storytelling aids memory, helps people make sense of complex information, and facilitates their passing along the story and its teachings to others.

Further, the book and the story are written so that everyone in a company — from the stockroom to the boardroom — can read it and have a common language within the company about its most important, organizational sustaining lifeblood: Positive Leadership.

How to Read This Book

Some people prefer to read the nonfiction part of the book (Part I) first in order to understand the theories and research at work before tackling the leadership fable (Part II). Other folks prefer to read the fable first and then explore the research. Whatever your preference, enjoy the read!

Foreword

At one time or another, we've all worked for good leaders and, unfortunately, bad ones. What separates these two is usually simple: Good ones make us feel positive, motivated and productive; however, bad ones do quite the opposite. Fortunately, thanks to the positive psychology movement led by Martin Seligman starting back in 1998 when he took the reins of the American Psychological Association, we've learned a lot about what makes people positive and productive. Thanks to research by Gallup, we know how engaged and positive employees dramatically impact the bottom line — in a big way. What's more, through the work of Richard Boyatzis, Daniel Goleman and Annie McKee, we know that leaders spread emotions — motivators — in the workplace with epidemic speed, infecting workers with either a positive (and productive) condition or a negative one.

In *Positive Leadership: The Game Changer at Work*, Steve Gladis — a respected executive coach, speaker, and author — offers leaders a double shot of positivity, written in two parts that combine into a memorable, easy-to-digest playbook for any leader. If you lead one person or one thousand, you'll want to read this book as quickly as you can and pass it on to someone you care about.

Marshall Goldsmith

Marshall Goldsmith has been recognized as the most influential leadership thinker in the world by Thinkers50 2011/HBR! He's also been recognized as one of the top ten most influential business thinkers in the global bi-annual study. www.marshallgoldsmith.com

Part I (The Concept)— Positive Leadership: The Game Changer at Work

Let's start off with a short, one-item, multiple-choice question:

What do most people want their children to be?

A. *Famous*

B. *Attractive*

C. *Wealthy*

D. *Happy*

If you're like most people, you chose "D. Happy."

Now, a follow-up:

So why, then, do so many people chase happiness by pursuing fame, glamour, and wealth?

Because of precisely that—they "pursue" happiness. For them, happiness is a goal or destination. They say to themselves, "If I only got that promotion, then I'd be happy." Or "If I got a facelift, then... ." These if-then statements that people tell themselves are delusional and wrongheaded.

For instance, happiness is typically conceptualized by researchers as a combination of mood—how you feel day-to-day—and overall life satisfaction—how you feel, all things considered (Deiner, 1999). *For the purposes of this book, I consider happiness as a state of mood and positivity as a state of mind.* While many things might make us happy—a sunny day, a smile, a compliment, a kind gesture, a friend, a child's voice, finishing a project, being inspired by a leader—it takes more to make us have a positive mindset. I'm reminded of the work by psychologist Carol Dweck at Stanford who talks about fixed and growth mindsets (Dweck, 2006), which I discuss later in the book, and of research by Barbara Frederickson, who discovered ten positive emotions leading to positivity (Fredrickson, 2009).

If you're a leader, you have a direct effect on the lives of others at a surprisingly powerful level. In short, you have great influence over both your own happiness and positivity and that of those around you.

So, while you'll see me use positivity and happiness together often in the same sentence — for ease of understanding — I'm really talking about both the mood of happiness and the mindset of positivity. My particular interest is not just the notions of positivity and happiness, but rather how positivity influences leaders who have a huge influence on others around them.

How exactly do leaders influence others? Gallup, the internationally renowned research firm, once asked more than 10,000 followers (note: Gallup asked followers, not leaders) the following questions (Rath & Conchie, 2009):

1. What leader has the most positive influence in your daily life?

2. List three words that best describe what this person contributes to your life.

The survey found that the words most frequently used to describe what great leaders brought to the lives of their followers clustered around the following four areas:

+ Trust

+ Compassion

+ Hope

+ Stability

That research tells me this: Followers want someone they can count on, not someone who can artificially pump sunshine into the room. Followers want leaders who will tell them the truth, be with them when the going gets tough, give them optimism and hope in the future, and keep the ship on an even keel.

According to research by Richard Boyatzis, distinguished professor of organizational behavior at Case Western Reserve University, mindfulness, compassion, and hope make leaders more in tune (resonant) with their followers. With co-author

Annie McKee, he wrote about this concept in *Resonant Leadership* (Harvard Business Review Press, 2005).

Resonance with followers makes a huge difference. Let me tell you a quick story of Phil and Bill. A long time ago I had a leadership job, and I was being led by a senior executive—Phil— who was open, playful, easy, and safe to talk to. He was competent, accomplished, happy, attentive, respectful, and humble. He was someone you could trust to always "have your back." I always felt I could bring both good and bad news to him, because he was compassionate, optimistic, and hopeful about whatever lay ahead. No matter the news, he either celebrated my team's wins or mourned our losses. He was right there with us, always adding support and stability. Above all, he trusted me and my team, and we trusted him right back—a genuine reciprocity. During his tenure as my boss, our team accomplished amazing results. People got awards, were promoted, and attracted others who wanted to work on such a high-performing team. And everyone wanted to work for Phil—especially me.

Then one day Phil got promoted and in came his replacement, Bill. Now, Bill was also competent and accomplished. But unlike Phil, Bill was, in my opinion, high-strung, judgmental, and distrusting. Bill came from an auditing-type of background. (Nothing against auditors, but with Bill you were guilty until proven innocent!) Trust was in short supply. I felt that he always treated me as if I had made an error somewhere, and he would try his best to find that mistake! In less than a month, my world changed from great to awful. I went from enjoying work to dreading it. In my opinion, Bill did not trust anyone. That lack of trust seemed to "infect" people who worked for him—it certainly affected me. Soon, my peers and I didn't trust each other, people coveted information, and they turned into "informants" on each other. I felt that, almost overnight, the place had become toxic. The result: Those of us who had options, including me, left as soon as we could.

The difference between Phil and Bill was simple: Phil had positivity, and Bill did not. And the research strongly suggests that positive leaders make all the difference and truly change the game.

This chapter will explore the importance of positivity in our lives and those we lead. Specifically, several questions will be answered:

1. What is positivity?
2. Why is positivity so important for leaders?
3. How can leaders increase positivity?

What Is Positivity?

Having scoured the research of psychologist-scholars who focus on positive mindsets—Martin Seligman, Barbara Frederickson, Shawn Achor, Tal Ben-Shahar, Sonja Lyubomirsky, and Ed Diener—here's my definition of positivity:

A mindset of positive mental wellbeing, meaning, and purpose.

Again, for the purposes of this book, consider happiness as a state of mood and positivity as a state of mind (mindset).

Positivity and Happiness

In her book, *The How of Happiness: A New Approach to Getting the Life You Want* (Penguin, 2008), professor and experimental psychologist Sonja Lyubomirsky gives us some potent statistics, especially when you analyze them in relation to each other. She has derived a formula for how we come to be happy, based on wide research by positive psychologists. The formula is as simple as it is powerful.

50-10-40

First, 50% of your happiness is inherited from your biological parents—Lyubomirsky calls this variance your genetic "set points." Thus, half of how happy you'll be got passed down through your gene pool. Studies on identical twins vs. fraternal twins support this finding. Lyubomirsky explains the variance by offering this analogy: Supposing you had a theater with 100 people, all of whom had identical DNA; you would still find variance in their set point levels of happiness. You cannot change that set point. As they say, it is what it is!

Second, all your life events and circumstances add up to only 10% of the variance in your happiness level. Even major events such as experiencing the death of a loved one, losing a job, filing for divorce, changing where you live, being assaulted, winning the lottery, losing a limb, and so on, only account for 10% of your happiness. So, blaming your parents, your school, or your lack of wealth as an excuse for why you are not happy only counts 10%! That's it. Some people have a hard time believing this, but scientists who study this phenomenon have the data.

Third, you control a full 40% of your own personal happiness. Much of your happiness lies, therefore, not in your genetic composition or your life circumstances, but in your personal behavior every day. Think about how big 40% is. If you owned 40% of a public company as a stockholder, whenever you came to an annual stockholders meeting, you'd be treated like a king! If you got a 40% pay raise, you'd be over the moon about it. If you were overweight and lost 40% of your weight, wow! You get the idea. In essence, 40% is a BIG number, and you have control over it.

Why Are Positivity and Happiness So Important to Leaders?

Our set points for happiness ultimately affect our overall positivity; so, what makes this critical for leaders? Some research on the nature of authority coupled with findings in neuroscience can help us understand this.

Authority

Authority has a powerful influence on followers: Leaders ARE the difference. They make the most difference because of their authority—for good or bad (Cialdini, 2009).

One classic study that highlighted this power of leaders over followers came in the form of a social science experiment at Yale in the 1960s. The Milgram experiment centered on obedience to authority figures. People designated as "learners" (wired with electrodes) sat in a booth removed from the "teachers," who were students at Yale and who were paid to participate. A lead "experimenter" in a lab coat, posing as a doctor, oversaw the experiment. Teachers were to ask the students questions. Whenever a learner got a question wrong, the teacher was to press a button that would give an electric shock to a learner. With each wrong answer, the shocks became incrementally more severe and evoked pleas from learners to cease the pain and suffering. Teachers (remember they were students) became overwrought because their punishing actions were in direct contrast with their social mores and values. However, at the insistence of the experimenter (the doctor in charge), the teachers administered the shocks to levels that would have killed learners.

Now, here's the rest of the story: The experimenter (the head authority figure) was not a real "doctor;" rather, he was an actor in the study about authority's effect on followers. Moreover, the "learners" were also actors, and the electrodes were not connected to any electrical currents—the actors just pretended to be shocked. The real purpose of this study was to isolate the effect of authority—to see how far healthy, well-adjusted, upper-middle-class students at Yale responded to authority. And the results? They acted just like the German Nazis who did terrible, unspeakable things to Jews in concentration camps but claimed (at the Nuremburg war trials) that they were just following orders from a higher authority. Though the Milgram experiment has come under some criticism for validity and ethics (Baumrind, 1964), it is a sad but amazing example of authority's power over us.

In yet another study (Cialdini, 2009), a similar phenomenon called "Captainitis" emerged. In a flight-simulator retraining experiment, captains were told by experimenters to do something catastrophic not long after the crew was "in flight." The "something" was to be not only catastrophic but also understood by the crew to be very dangerous. Despite the fact that crews knew what had happened could potentially kill them and the passengers, 25% of the crews—one in every four—said nothing to challenge the captain.

There are numerous other examples in daily life about authority's influence. Just look at the power and influence that CEOs, hospital doctors, teachers, ministers, priests, coaches, and many others have over people who report to them. The newspapers are full of examples of just how that power can be misused.

Neuroscience: Our Brain—An Open System

In recent years, neuroscience has opened up the brain's secrets. Unlike our circulatory, muscular, pulmonary, skeletal, or respiratory systems, which are closed systems, our brains are open systems. Our brains are hard-wired to warn us of potential harm or threats in the environment. In the middle of our brains, for example, resides an almond-shaped primal mechanism called the amygdala. (Technically there are two amygdalae, one in the right and left hemispheres of the brain. However, since they work like identical twins simultaneously, scientists treat these two as one, thus use the term amygdala).

The amygdala serves as the brain's smoke detector. It's always on, always picking up signals, especially from the leader. As part of the limbic system (our primitive, ancient brain), the amygdala stimulates the injection of hormones for fight or flight into the body, activating the sympathetic nervous system.

Here is the basic question that the amygdala needs to have answered: Will this threat eat me, or can I eat it (Goleman, 2007)! As long as we see something as a threat, we will focus on it intently, which narrows our scope, creativity, and ability to think of creative solutions (Boyatzis & McKee, 2005). In contrast, our normal, relaxed peripheral vision offers about 180 degrees of lateral panoramic vision: We need only rotate our heads modestly to see all around us. In karate it's called "soft eyes" and allows confident and calm black belts to "see" attacks coming at them from anywhere in the room.

Unfortunately, when we get overstressed through the grind of threat after threat in our fast-paced world, we tend to invest more and more of ourselves (The Sacrifice Syndrome) to keep things afloat (Boyatzis & McKee, 2005) . Eventually, all that stress pushes us into a state of negativity called "dissonance." Dissonance produces poor judgment, disharmony, and ultimately dysfunction (Boyatzis). Under these conditions, our visual field can narrow to as little as 30 degrees, depending on the severity of the threat. We get fixated only on what's right in front of us — often making poor decisions — because we lack the advantages of peripheral vision (greater data input). You might recall the movie *Jurassic Park* and how the dangerous raptors hunted prey. One raptor shows up in front of the prey, whose focus then shrinks to 30 degrees — its eyes are understandably riveted on the creature getting ready to attack — essentially freezing the prey in its tracks. Then, suddenly and surprisingly, the second raptor attacks from the side and kills the prey, precisely because the prey is fixated only on the raptor right in front of it.

When we're in dissonance we're fixated on "the threat" (not necessarily simply a physical threat; the threat could be a complaint, an overdue report, a missed sales quota, etc.). And in the state of dissonance caused by constant stress, we are literally out of tune! One sure-fire test of whether or not a leader is in the state of dissonance: The leader thinks that s/he's surrounded by "jerks" who don't pull their own weight — in contrast to the leader, of course!

Unfortunately, dissonance is not some rare leadership disease. Rather, Boyatzis says, dissonance is the "default" for all of us. Why? Because the amygdala is always on aler, wired into our brains. As leaders we must work to cou, dissonance default because its effects on everyone are stagge, Stress creates "tunnel vision" and makes leaders vulnerable t, huge judgment errors and mistakes. Dissonant leaders jump to conclusions, get defensive, and create stress both in themselves and in others. Comedian Danny Thomas once said that he knew a woman whose favorite position was "beside herself" and whose favorite sport was "jumping to conclusions." She was clearly in a state of dissonance!

Because of their power of authority, leaders are like WiFi "hot spots" you might find at places such as Panera's or Starbucks. Such leadership hot spots broadcast a strong signal, which gets picked up by roaming wireless network connectors in the brains of followers. When leaders are far away, like our WiFi connectors or cell phones, we only feel one or two "bars" of reception. Their influence is not as strong. But when they're close, raise their voices, or display emotion, our brains magnify their output. Our "receptivity" is five bars strong. It's been said that leaders don't have voices—they have megaphones or amplifiers. In fact, leaders set the weather (mood) of the workplace and over time can change the climate (personality) of the organization. Thus, working around a depressed leader can depress you. Work around a positive leader, and you get positive (Goleman, Boyatzis, & McKee, 2004).

Some theorists say that we affect people at least three levels "out" beyond ourselves. Think about the last time your son or daughter was deeply hurt by someone and brought that emotional baggage home to you, and then you told your spouse or friend, and so on. Depending on the severity of the incident, any number of people are affected by the original transgression—the influence of which grows geometrically over time. Indeed, leaders create an emotional wake and a contagion that can spread either as a positive force or a negative virus (Goleman, Boyatzis, & McKee, 2004).

kicker: Good or bad, leaders have a strong
...ods, emotions, and productivity. Negativ-
...ement and *a 30% lack of productivity* (Buck-

...nd, positive leaders spread a mood of trust
and ...h can lead to creativity and cognitive ease—
the ability to think without restraints and consider a number of
options to solve important problems reflectively, rather than by
overreacting (Kahneman, 2011). Psychologist and professor Barbara Frederickson at the University of North Carolina espouses
a theory called "broaden and build." Agreeing that stress creates "tunnel vision" that makes us vulnerable to huge judgment
errors and mistakes, Frederickson's broaden-and-build schema
positivity creates a safe place and opens up the mind, which allows us to listen, learn, and solve problems better and faster.

What's the Science of Positivity?

For many years, psychologists have studied mental illness such
as depression (reaction to loss), anxiety (reaction to a threat), and
anger (reaction to trespass), with great success, which has been
psychology's legacy and its curse. Success often leads us to rep-
lication. If we have success doing something, we tend to want
to repeat it, even if another approach might work better, especially as the world changes. Thus, experimental psychologists
kept studying mental disease and how to cure it. They essentially
continued to study illness rather than health, so they knew more
about what made us sick than about what kept us healthy. In
fact, in 1998 the ratio of negative to positive psychology research
articles published was 17:1 (Achor, 2010).

However, also in 1998, psychologist Martin Seligman became the chairman of the American Psychological Association
and announced that under his chairmanship "positive psychology" would become a central tenet of the association's strategy.
(Indeed, one could easily call Marty Seligman the "Father of

Positive Psychology.") Instead of studying what went wrong, the association was called to study what went right.

Consider the metaphor of a number line that represents illness and health, with "0" being the turning point from one to the other.

Prior to Seligman, psychology only got us to "0" (zero — a normal, neutral state of no depression; Seligman, 2012). However, a lack of depression is not happiness, nor does it create a state of positivity any more than the lack of fear is the presence of courage. Positive psychology, as Seligman defined it, was about getting from 0 to +10 .

Today, we can count more than 200 studies (involving more than 275,000 people) on happiness. A meta-analysis of those studies showed happiness to have a significant effect on relationships at work and home as well as on health and nearly every significant life domain. In short, happiness (the mood that leads to the mindset of positivity) is good medicine for us all (Achor, 2010).

Here are some examples of the research in positive psychology:

+ **Productivity:** A meta-analysis of 225 academic studies revealed that happy employees are 31% more productive, produce 37% more in sales, and are 300% (three times) more creative than their unhappy colleagues (Lyubomirsky, 2008).

+ **Depression:** A Conference Board study found that only 45% people like their jobs. We have ten times the amount of depression as we did in 1960 (Achor, 2010).

+ **Employee engagement:** Gallup revealed that only 20% of the work population is actively engaged at work. This sets up a powerful equation of loss that creates a tremendous "silent economic killer" to any company (Buckingham, 2005).

The Return on Investment (ROI) of Positivity

Let's do the math and calculate the impact of the "silent killer" of negativity to corporations, no matter their size. If we accept the research by these accomplished scientists, the risk isn't just serious, but profound. It means *that 80% of the entire workforce is producing 31% less than what they are capable of.* Therefore, our workforce is potentially under-producing by a whopping 24%! Here's what that means, depending on the size of your organization:

✚ For a $1B corporation, the productivity loss is $240 million!

✚ For a $100M corporation, the productivity loss is $24 Million!

✚ For a $10M corporation, the productivity loss is $2.4 Million!

Those are huge losses! The figures are also a clue about how to get a huge boost in profits: by having leaders take specific actions to increase their company's ROI.

In short, increase the level of positivity, increase the bottom line.

How Can Leaders Increase Positivity?

Positivity starts with the leader. My review of the research leads me to what might be called "creating a positive mindset." The collective findings can be expressed in three simple steps. To increase positivity, and consequently productivity, leaders should:

1. **Get Social** in their relationships.
2. **Get Strong** at work.
3. **Get Positive** in their activities.

To help better explain these three major influencers of positivity, I'll use a "Leadership Positivity Matrix." Hopefully, it will help you understand and be able to apply positivity to your particular workplace.

The Leadership Positivity Matrix

What can leaders do to create positivity at work? The Leadership Positivity Matrix (below) provides a brief overview about how leaders can influence positivity for themselves and their teams. Here's the matrix template that will be filled out as we proceed:

The Positive Leadership Matrix

How of Positivity	Step#1: Get Social	Step #2: Get Strong	Step #3: Get Positive
Who of Positivity: Leaders			

Step 1: Get Social in Your Relationships

We are all social animals who thrive on relationships with those around us. Engaging in significant relationships will especially ground leaders in reality. Such engaged relationships help leaders increase their own positivity, even in the face of the inevitable daily pressures of life. A review of the research reveals that for any leader there are three important relationships: family, friends, and coworkers (which includes bosses, peers, and direct reports).

Engage Your Family

The core element of social stability for anyone is the family — it's the ultimate team. Leaders who have grounded family relationships get the regular support they need to face the many challenges that they confront daily at work.

Some of the more remarkable research in the relationship between positivity and family comes from the research conducted by Marcel Losada (Fredrickson, 2009). Though Losada studied working teams, groups, and boards of businesses in a laboratory-type setting, what he found applies directly to our fundamental team—the family. His research has been reviewed, studied, and endorsed by other leaders in this field.

Losada watched the way leaders and individuals acted with each other. He found that the ratios of positive-negative interpersonal interactions predicted the level of success that teams and individuals would experience in dealing with others.

To have a flourishing, healthy relationship, Losada found that people (especially leaders) need a ratio of 3:1 positive-to-negative interactions with others. People who experienced three positive reactions for every negative reaction they received could keep their relationships positive. Put another way, for every slight or criticism they levied, leaders need three positive interactions (comments, emails, non-verbal gestures, etc.) to keep relationships with others (especially family) pointed toward the positive zone. (Negative interactions are far more powerful and damaging than positive interactions.)

Here are a few more of Losada's ratios to consider:

+ A 2:1 positive-to-negative ratio of interactions produces a flat-line relationship—a relationship remains basically unaffected and flat—neither moving up or down in terms of positivity. Again this ratio reflects clearly that negative interactions (comments, emails, non-verbal gestures, etc.) have twice the power of positive interactions.

+ A 1:1 positive-to-negative ratio represents a relationship headed for divorce or breakup.

Simply put, to enjoy a flourishing relationship, people need far more positivity than negativity.

What about if you're married? Hold onto your hats on this one! Marriage researcher John Gottman—professor emeritus at the University of Washington—was made famous in Malcom Gladwell's popular book, *Blink: The Power of Thinking Without Thinking* (Little, Brown, & Co., 2007). For many years Gottman put married couples in a room and gave them scenarios involving a disagreement. He and his researchers watched how the couples argued. Over time, they began to be able to remarkably predict (an 80% success rate) how long marriages will last in as few as fifteen minutes. If periods of observation are increased significantly, the predictive rate reached 95%.

Gottman identified what he called the "Four Horsemen of the Apocalypse": Criticism, Contempt, Defensiveness, and Stonewalling.

+ **Criticism** focuses on taking pot shots at your mate's personality, rather than focusing on the behavior. It sounds like this: "You're acting like a real jerk."

+ **Contempt** is criticism on steroids and has a massive effect on damaging relationships. This can involve eye rolling, deep sighs (and other negative non-verbals), sarcasm, and direct personal attacks, such as saying, "You're an idiot."

+ **Defensiveness** is not only a response to attack and conflict, but it also can corrode a relationship. Offering excuses, shifting blame, name calling, or swearing and fighting back (counter-attacking) are examples of defensiveness.

+ **Stonewalling** is a direct refusal to engage in a conflict by not responding to someone's comments or by just walking away. While this is OK at times, continuous stonewalling in response to conflict will take down a relationship or marriage. While all relationships and marriages at times involve these four horsemen, when they become the default responses of your relationship, it's headed for tough sailing and likely divorce.

So what is Gottman's advice? You need a 5:1 positive-to-negative ratio of interactions with your spouse! That's right—5:1. Asked for his single best piece of advice after thirty years of research in this field, Gottman told a writer from the *Harvard Business Review* to just simply say "yes" to most everything (Coutu, 2007). What he means is for people in relationships to start from "yes" (a positive state) and not from "no" (a negative state). So when a spouse asks, "Do you want to go out to dinner?" unless you're in physically debilitating pain or the president of the United States has called you for your opinion, Gottman's theory might suggest you say, "Yes, that sounds like a good idea!"(Pretty simple, yet pretty tough to remember and employ in daily life.) It's like playing golf. While we may intellectually know how to swing the club, it takes an enormous amount of practice to actually play the game consistently and reliably well. However, if you do practice saying "yes," marriage, like golf, gets easier and better.

An interesting note: Marty Seligman is working with the U.S. Army to reduce marital and family conflict and other serious outcomes of combat exposure, to include the ultimate issue, suicide (Seligman, 2012). Today's war fighter not only has to contend with a life-threatening enemy but also with the pressure of being in constant contact with his or her family via email and even Skype, a level of communication never available to soldiers previously. This can be both an advantage and a stressor at the same time, such as when a spouse back home complains about the soldier's absence. The pressure of dealing with both serious combat and domestic threats simultaneously can be overwhelming for some soldiers.

Engage Your Friends

Good friends can act as "sounding boards" by listening to you and asking good questions. For day-to-day issues, a good friend who will listen to you provides great value. A listening, attentive friend can provide the just-in-time ability for you to tell your story — whatever's on your mind. The value of this should be neither under- nor overstated. However valuable the support that an attentive friend can give, your friend isn't trained in psycho-therapy or coaching. (You do get what you pay for. But if you want to find a good sounding board, ask a friend.)

How good a sounding board is that friend? Ask yourself the following questions: Does my friend listen without interrupting me? Is s/he empathetic? When I'm hurting does s/he focus on me or turn the conversation back to being about himself/herself? Is our relationship reciprocal—I listen, and my friend listens? Note: Friends are not as good a sounding board as trained therapists for a host of reasons, not the least of which is a lack of training in identifying key psychological and or mental illnesses that might need a specific standard of care to solve the issue. That said, talking to a sympathetic friend has great benefits over taking counsel solely from yourself!

To develop a strong, supportive friend, you, too, will need to invest time, energy, and emotion into that relationship. Surely compassion and empathy are limited founts within us all. In fact, British researcher and anthropologist Robin Dunbar posits that based on the size of the average human neo-cortex, people can only maintain social relationships with up to 150 people—often called Dunbar's Number (Dunbar, 1992). Beyond that you need far more of a bureaucracy with rules and structure to easily keep track of relationships. Certain companies in fact will only build structures that hold 150 people. One such company uses the following indicator as a signal to build a new building: It constructs a parking lot that accommodates 150 cars, and when people regularly start having to park on the grass, the company starts to plan the next building (Gladwell, 2002).

Engage Your Co-Workers

When at work, think about "360-degree positivity." Most people, especially executives, know what a 360 assessment is. Coaches or HR managers collect data on an employee to aid that person in increased self-awareness—learning how others see the employee, not as the employee thinks others see him/her. Specific questions are asked of a range of people at varying levels (peers, direct reports, boss) who know the employee being assessed. Their responses to the questions are aggregated and fed back to the employee as a way of having a clear image of how s/he "presents" or "shows up" to others.

To apply the 360-degree concept to positivity, consider your primary work relationships: your immediate boss, your peers, and your direct reports. Apply various techniques that you learn in this book to them all and watch relationships improve. Consider the following actions:

Engage your boss. Your direct supervisor, your boss, can make your work life fun and engaging or miserable and a chore; so, take time to get to know him or her. Daniel Goleman, emotional intelligence guru, tells us that, outside of our immediate family, our relationship with our boss is one of the most critical in our lives. Goleman calls the relationship the "Vertical Couple" (Goleman, 2007). This hierarchical coupling can be one of beauty or one of the beast—one of pleasure or pain. And that relationship can change overnight with the entrance of a new boss. (Recall the Phil and Bill story I offered at the outset of this book!)

Finding out what makes your boss tick is one of your primary jobs, especially at the beginning of a new relationship. Also, if s/he sees you as an asset and not as a potential threat, you'll be much better off. Indeed, trying to identify similarities between you will start you on the path to "liking" that Bob Cialdini notes in *Influence* is critical to any relationship, especially the one you have with your boss. Cialdini states that we like people who are similar to us, and we tend to like people who like us. So, demonstrate your similarity to and your liking for your boss.

Similarity might be found in a hobby, interest, or sport you both enjoy. It's like when you were "courting" someone you found attractive. When most people meet in a courting situation, they try to find connections among things they enjoy in common, like movies, places lived, and music. If you want this boss–direct report relationship to work, start finding ways to connect with your boss and to add value to him or her from day one.

Engage your peers. Professional colleagues make a real difference in how positive your work life can be. Often neglected, this "stealth force" of positivity and happiness on the job should be harnessed. Remember, peers will watch you very carefully to see if you're a threat or a benefit to the culture—and to them. Take the time to cultivate peers—as colleagues, not competitors. Recall the concept of "liking" mentioned above. It's far more important that your peers see you as a positive addition, not as a threat—especially within your first several months at your organization.

Despite what your boss or the HR director might say up front, such as, "This place needs to be shaken up," remember to shake very gently at the beginning, or you'll be shaken out of the organization! Cultures take years to form. They "protect" the organization's survival, and neither you nor any policy will change that unless someone's willing to fire the entire team—which is highly unlikely. Peers can and do help you succeed or fail, equally.

So proceed with care and take a "learning attitude" right from the beginning. Rather than assume you have more experience than anyone, assume you know nothing and ask a lot of questions. This might be difficult because you'll be tempted to impress peers by showing them all you know—i.e., how smart you are. That would be unwise. Consider yourself a consultant: Ask many questions to figure out the culture, people, processes, and technologies. Again, getting peers to see you as value added rather than as a threat is critical to your success. Here are some ways to accomplish that:

✛ Compliment peers sincerely whenever you have the opportunity.

✛ Share the stage and the limelight with them whenever you can.

✛ Invite them to lunch so you can learn about them, their team, and the company.

✛ Invest time and energy into the relationship to get real results.

Things to *definitely avoid:*

✛ The "white horse" hero syndrome. Don't present yourself as a hero, as someone who will help them finally "get it."

✛ The "me" and "I" trap when speaking. Make it a we/us, not an I/me, conversation.

✛ The "it's all about me" syndrome. Make it about them, not you. This is harder to do than it sounds but worth the effort in the long term.

✛ Egotism of any sort.

✛ Always taking credit for accomplishments.

Engage your direct reports. Relationships make the difference between engaged and disengaged employees (who most definitely will help or block you from succeeding). Gallup's research in the area of employee engagement provides the benchmark for success. Gallup has collected data now from millions of participants using its Q-12 questionnaire, designed to measure engagement (and positivity) in the workplace. The researchers have developed twelve critical questions that measure whether employees like and are engaged in their work. The twelve questions correlate with a positive mindset. Key words found embedded within the twelve questions are as follows: Praise, friend, caring, encouragement, working at what you're best at, and others, all focused on creating a positive, engaged mindset. By Gallup's measure, only about 20% of all employees are working in strength areas most of the time.

As you already know, one of the most critical engagement questions is the "vertical relationship" between employee and supervisor (Goleman, Boyatzis, & McKee, 2004). A survey of 19,500 executives say they left their company because of a bad boss (senior executive). However, when asked, those bosses were completely unaware of why their employees had left and told researchers that they believed the employees had left for better pay and advancement. Not so! Let's be very clear: People leave bosses, not jobs (Cashman, 2008)!

You want to be the kind of boss who engages your employees, because at the very least, engaged employees are far more productive—a whopping 30% more productive! They also miss less work, are more supportive, and have less absenteeism than less-engaged employees—and they bolster a sense of optimism (Buckingham, 2005). In *First Break All the Rules*, Buckingham noted that lack of engagement costs a company an overall loss of 24% in productivity (80% of the people under-producing by 30%). Do the math on what that costs for your company by simply multiplying 24% by your gross income. The numbers are staggering.

Engage the team. At work, we're expected to serve on all manner of teams—cross-functional, virtual, matrixed, and others. Caring about another person, especially the people on your team, is at the core of positivity and happiness. In fact, caring, almost above all else, often becomes the major differentiator between fair or poor leaders and good or great ones. In a previous book, *The Trusted Leader* (HRD Press, 2011), I explored this concept in what I call the Trust Triangle—Good Character, Good Sense, and Goodwill—words used by Aristotle to describe a trustworthy person. In modern terminology, we might use three C's: Character, Competence, and Caring. Let's consider what the research tells us about what followers, in general, want from leaders. Then we'll look at what teams need for success.

As mentioned at the very beginning of this chapter, Gallup surveyed more than 10,000 people to determine, as followers, what they most prized in a leader. To do this, they asked only two simple but powerful questions:

+ What leader has the most positive influence in your daily life?

+ List three words that best describe what this person contributes to your life.

After all the data came in, authors Tom Rath and Barry Conchie in their book *Strengths-Based Leadership: Great Leaders, Teams, and Why People Follow* (Gallup Press, 2009) revealed Gallup's important findings. Those findings validated the research and writing of people like Boyatzis, Goleman, and others about what followers wanted from their leaders:

1. **Trust**: Honesty, respect, and integrity

2. **Compassion**: Caring, friendship, happiness, and love

3. **Hope**: Direction, faith, and guidance

4. **Stability**: Security, strength, support, and peace

By now most of these characteristics should look familiar. Unfortunately, such noble characteristics are not always the ones associated with our leaders. Poor leaders can create as much abuse — or even more — as good leaders can create decency and kindness. Moreover, whether it is abuse or kindness, a leader's behavior spreads with equal speed and ferocity. One person — particularly the leader of a team — can change the mood and atmosphere toward collaboration, satisfaction, and productivity or toward a more negative pole of internal competition, dissatisfaction, and a lack of engagement and productivity.

We are social creatures who depend on each other for strength, happiness, and energy. At their very essence, organizations are an aggregate of complex relationships, including teams. Again, Gallup discovered critical aspects about healthy, balanced teams that were reported by Rath and Conchie, organized into four key domains:

1. **Strategic Thinking**: A focus on patterns, the future, on over-arching ideas

2. **Influence**: The ability to sell team ideas within and outside the organization

3. **Relationship Building**: The social glue that bonds people, teams, clients

4. **Execution**: The ability to get things done

No single person will necessarily have all four of these domains, but teams should have balance — members with strengths in all four areas. The bottom line: Whenever possible, hire toward balanced teams and engage people's strengths toward the team's mission. Just as leaders must get social for their own development, so too they must pay attention to those they lead, especially teams.

Respect the pack. It's no startling surprise to find out that we are all social or "pack" animals, each belonging to our tribes, whatever we call them — families, companies, churches, or political parties. However, David Brooks, vaunted *New York Times* journalist and author of *The Social Animal: The Hidden Sources of Love, Character, and Achievement* (Random House Trade Paperbacks, 2011), scrapes off the layers of paint atop that old truism down to its bare metal, exposing three key insights: (1) the power of the unconscious; (2) the centrality of emotions; and (3) the deep interpenetration and interconnectedness of our minds. Brooks raises the old Greek notion that we "suffer our way to wisdom." Brooks discusses skills that operate below the level of consciousness, as we play out these three insights of unconsciousness, emotions, and interconnectedness.

Teams at work play out Brooks' thinking every day. To understand the impact of positivity, you might consider the results of positivity on a group or team setting. First, positive teams outperform individuals almost every time. In only the rarest of instances is that not true, for example in an emergency when there is an expert standing right there at the switch. But when there's time to think, reflect, and make excellent long-term decisions with major impact, go with the team. Moreover, positive teams regularly outperform teams riddled with negativity and disengagement.

What specifically can leaders do to help teams get and remain positive?

+ **Ask and listen**: First and foremost, use the coach-approach to leadership (Gladis, 2012). This approach requires leaders to do two things well: First, ask probing questions, prompted by listening with real curiosity, and second, resist trying to solve other people's problems. Let's cover these briefly.

   Ask probing questions: Ask questions that cause people to reflect, such as Who, How, What, and Open-Ended Questions. What's going on? How does that work? Can you give me an example? Who's involved in this situation? Avoid yes-or-no questions.

   Focus on four critical areas to help others solve any problem: (1) The Issue (What's the real problem here?); (2) The Impact (Who and how are people being affected today?); (3) The Ideal Future State (What would it look like if all was perfect in the future?); (4) The Intention (Going forward, what do you plan to do by when?)

   Resist trying to solve other people's problems: Most of us during our life have been rewarded for the having the right, correct answer. In school and on the job, you get "gold stars" and pay raises for having the right answers. Consequently, we become the answer-man or answer-woman. The compulsion to give advice remains our default and a very tough habit to overcome. So develop "alligator arms." Think about how short an alligator's arms are and simulate that when people try to hand you their problems to solve. If you develop alligator arms, you won't be able to take other's problems. This lack of taking on their problems actually empowers them by forcing them to confront their own problems.

+ **Communicate intentionally**: Business processes help keep us on track. If you value something, you need to build a process around it to ensure it gets done. I've mentioned before Susan Scott's great quote ("The conversation is the relationship."). Because communication is a core element in all human relationships, positive leaders will want to take heed and get very intentional about organizational communication. I know of no simpler or more effective system than the one Pat Lencioni suggests in his book, *Death by Meeting: A Leadership Fable...About Solving the Most Painful Problem in Business* (Jossey-Bass, 2004). Using his system will ensure the rapid, useful, and systematic communication required for high-performing teams. Here's what Lencioni suggests:

+ Daily check-in meeting with your team. This meeting is done at the same time, only if you're there, and if it takes more than five minutes, you've taken too long. Ask everyone to share one or two key issues of the day—no discussion, just info.

+ Weekly tactical meetings. These are agenda-less. Conduct a "lightning round" where participants take no more than two minutes or so to discuss their top three priorities. After that, the leader drills down asking questions about the most important ones that emerge. Figure on an hour for this meeting.

+ Monthly strategic meetings. These have an agenda and focus on strategic issues that impact on the near-term and long-term vision/strategy of the company. The leader frames the issue to be discussed and announces it and the agenda before the meeting.

✚ Quarterly off-site review. This should take one to two days, if possible, away from the office and phones and email. These meetings tackle big picture stuff like succession, strategy review, team building, and leadership development.

So, let's turn to The Positive Leadership Matrix to keep track of where we are:

How of Positivity	Step#1: Get Social	Step #2: Get Strong	Step #3: Get Positive
Who of Positivity: Leaders can influence	**Personal Life:** Family Friends **Professional Life:** Boss Peers Direct Reports Teams **Engage the Team**		

Step 2: Get Strong at Work

Nobody ever became successful focused on his or her weaknesses. Sure, it's helpful to patch holes in our lives that tend seriously to hurt us—so-called "fatal flaws" that repeatedly jump up and bite us. For example, arrogance must be dealt with before it drags us into dysfunctional relationships with people who matter, like family, bosses, and coworkers. Developing time management strategies for someone who's chronically late with projects and easily distracted makes sense before s/he gets shown to the door.

But if creativity is the person's secret ingredient, figuring out how to take it to the next level (rather than becoming expert at time management) is really where the big payoff for growth is. In fact, I'd argue that it might be cheaper to hire an assistant to "patch" that time management challenge. There's a great saying in the U.S. Marine Corps: "Never try to teach a pig how to sing. You won't be successful, and you'll just piss off the pig!"

Know Your Strengths

Here's one truth that you can take to the bank and deposit: People have strengths and challenges. It's the human condition that we ALL possess incredible strengths and often complementary challenges—just by being human! As a leader, finding out "what you're good at" is the starting place for all happiness and positivity. Fortunately, a number of researchers and writers have pondered this strengths-and-challenges question and can provide guidance in acquiring self-knowledge to anyone willing to take a valid and reliable diagnostic instrument. Here are just a few of the most popular:

+ **360-Degree Assessment:** Available in any number of forms, 360s are by far the most in-vogue instruments that organizations use today to give feedback from their peers, direct reports, and boss to leaders. Whether paper-and-pencil or web-based, these instruments elicit honest and anonymous feedback about strengths and challenges on a wide variety of leadership areas. Feedback sessions with a trained facilitator usually are part of the service. Unfortunately, following receipt of their assessment, most people focus on their challenges rather than strengths. Remember that people go from good to great by shoring up any major challenges but mostly by exploiting their strengths.

+ **Meyers Briggs Type Indicator (MBTI):** This instrument measures the psychometrics of how people vary in the way they get their psychological energy, gather data, make decisions, and view the world. The theory helps people understand how their individual personality gifts can be used to maximize their contribution and satisfaction. Developed by two women, Katharine Briggs and her daughter Isabel Briggs Myers, the MBTI was originally focused on how to help other women enter the wartime workforce of WWII. Based on personality-type theories of famed Swiss psychologist, Carl Jung and his book *Psychological Types: The Collected Works of C. G. Jung* (Princeton University Press, 1976), this instrument is one of the most widely used of its kind in industry today.

+ **StrengthsFinder**: The Gallup StrengthsFinder is a web-based personality assessment tool that is focused on positive psychology. Using 180 pairs of questions arranged to make the participant choose between two preferences, ultimately the instrument measures thirty-four general areas called "themes." This established theory posits that people behave, choose, and react according to their unique talents, which serve as the basis for practice and development into true strengths.

+ **DISC**: A personal assessment instrument designed to help people understand each other, communicate better, form teams, and make decisions. The instrument produces a report that indicates preferences for Dominance, Influence, Steadiness, and Conscientiousness. Dominant personalities focus on getting things done, taking action and challenging themselves and others. Dominant people seek results and are both direct and competitive. Influencers seek to sway or persuade others and focus on social recognition, approval, and having purpose and meaning. Steady personalities like to cooperate to get things done in a calm, patient, humble, and team-oriented way. Conscientious people work well with rules and toward being accurate, clear, and concise.

✛ **Values in Action Signature Strengths**: This instrument was developed by father of positive psychology Martin Seligman. It measures twenty-four character strengths.

While it's not certain which one of these instruments is better than the next, what is certain is that knowing your preferences and strengths will help you lead a happier, healthier, and more fulfilled life. Not a bad return on investment.

Work with Your Strengths, or "Work-In" Your Strengths

Let's see how knowing your personality might be "worked into" your job. Without going into a complete recitation of the MBTI, here's a simple look at how it works — using two of the four scales of personality. And, these two scales taken together are the "cognitive elements," or how we think — i.e., how we process information and decide on it:

1. How we *process information*

   a. **Sensors** are data-focused people who collect and analyze data well. They're good with detail, analysis, and tactical thinking. In MBTI parlance they're referred to as S's.

   b. **iNtuitors** (not a misprint!) tend to focus on the "big picture" and look at data as a jumping off point to connect, process, and synthesize new information. They're good at concepts, synthesis, and strategic thinking. In MBTI parlance, they're referred to as N's.

2. How we *make decisions* on the information we collect:

   c. **Thinkers** use structured logic to make decisions on the data they possess. They value structure, order, and logic. In MBTI parlance, they are called T's.

   d. **Feelers** use values, mores, and customs to make decisions about the data they possess. The put a high premium on people, culture, and harmony. In MBTI parlance they're called F's.

Four cognitive types result from the combinations of these elements: STs, SFs, NFs, and NTs:

+ **ST's — Sensor Thinkers**: Good at hard-nosed data collection, tactics, and analysis. They make decisions based on data and logic and are less concerned with people than with data. This cognitive type (ST) personality often shows up in all professions but especially in professions like accounting, technology, and business administration.

+ **SF's — Sensor Feelers**: Good at data, tactics, and working with people. They make decisions on the strength of the data as it relates to the people or group they're working with. This cognitive type (SF) personality shows up in every profession but especially as teachers, administrators, and coaches.

+ **NF — iNtuitive Feelers**: Good at big-picture thinking, strategy, and working with people, they make decision on the strength of their ideas and concepts as these ideas and concepts relate to people. This cognitive type (NF) personality often shows up in all professions but especially in professions like education, journalism, and influence professions.

+ **NT — iNtuitive Thinkers**: Good at big-picture thinking, strategy, and logic. They make decisions on the strength of their strategic thinking. This cognitive type (NT) personality often shows up in all professions, but especially often in professions related to science, education, and business.

Here's an example of how personality affects work: If you, an NF, were to take a job that required working with mounds of data, dealing with intensive detail, and without anyone to influence—that type of job might drive you nuts! However, if you were to become a teacher or trainer, where you dealt with influencing people, working with big and important issues, receiving good feedback—then, you'd most likely be in heaven.

Thus, the value in finding out early on what your likes and dislikes are and matching them as closely as possible to your job is critical for your personal happiness. And after all, that's what most of us want in life. But what happens when you have to eat and pay your bills, and the only job you can get for now is not the best match for your talents?

That's when you have to "work-in" your talents to the job. As the old song goes: *If you can't be with the one you love, love the one you're with!* Well not quite! But simply put, you have to adapt your talents to the job—especially if you need the money. Again, an example might help.

Let's say you, an NF, have to take that detail-oriented job— the one that required working with tons of data, dealing with detail, and without anyone to influence. Such a job might well distress you; how could you "work-in" your strengths? Here are a few suggestions:

+ Volunteer to teach or train others at a nonprofit, church, or other organization to get your "teaching fix."

+ Develop tactics to hone your detail-proofing skills. One technique is to read things backwards or change fonts when self-editing. Also, take frequent short breaks.

+ Conduct your work at a local Starbucks or at other gathering places when or if you need people for energy. The ambient social energy will help you be more productive.

+ Use Skype or Facetime to "meet virtually" with others. In essence, create virtual office mates, which you can turn on and click off whenever you like!

+ Set your own deadlines and timelines and keep score, especially if you're competitive.

+ Volunteer to coach the company softball team, produce the corporate newsletter, or staff any off-line jobs that feed your passions.

I hope you get the idea that if you're not where you want to be, it's up to you to figure out the best alternative, short of quitting and hitting the unemployment lines. Remember to work-in your strengths if you want to be as happy as you can be until you find the job that's the right fit for you.

Make Work a "Calling"

The best-case scenario: You'll eventually be able to find work that matches your strengths.

My recommended ratio for the ideal job is to find an 80:20 strengths-to-challenges ratio match. If you can spend 80% of your time working in your areas of high interest, talent, and strength, work will be fun, creative, and fulfilling. But remember that even the best-matched work will have things associated with it that just have to get done — like filing taxes, sending out invoices, and paying bills (this is somewhat autobiographical here!).

Research conducted at Yale University (Lyubomirsky, 2008) indicates that people have three views or mindsets about work. Some look at their labor as a job, others view it as a career, and finally, some see their work as a calling.

+ **A job**: Those who see their daily labor as a job consider it strictly a way to make a living that allows them to do the things they really like to do, such as playing golf, running, or just reading a book under a tree. Such folks work in order to pay the rent, tuition, and bills. They watch the clock like hawks, often to find out that time moves ever so slowly when they're not engaged in their work and merely marking time to collect a paycheck. These folks love Fridays and hate Mondays! If you're a person with a "job," it often feels like you're in jail, waiting for parole every day at 5 P.M.

✦ **A career**: Those who see their work as a career strive to climb the career ladder to get to the next rung of success. They don't watch the clock like people with "jobs." Rather, career-oriented workers watch the calendar. For them, developing a career has certain calendar-centric milestones. Often, career-oriented people know approximately when they'll become a manager, a district supervisor, or a vice-president. They often compare their success to that of their peers. It's as if their career were a race and a promotion the prize—an objective to be sought and coveted like a gold medal at the Olympics.

✦ **A calling**: Those who see their work as a calling view their work as truly making a difference—a noble, inspired activity that puts a ding or dent in the universe. Work is their vocation—they do what they love, and they love what they do. Ask a person with a "calling" what s/he might do in retirement, and it's often to volunteer doing exactly what they do in their current profession. Retired teachers who love teaching, for example, volunteer to teach at churches, non-profits, and even jails. These folks neither watch the clock nor watch the calendar but work with a sense of urgency and importance as if their hair were on fire! A police officer who feels a sense of "calling," for instance, might deeply want to make life better and safer for a kid going to school in a tough neighborhood.

Here's a frequent question asked about this concept: Is having a calling associated with a certain profession, training or education, or position in a company?

No.

There are janitors and school bus drivers who were once in business and industry and now just enjoy the "calling" of making a school room or school bus a safe place to help kids get their education. For folks working in their calling, attending to their basic duties (like sweeping a floor or driving a bus) becomes important and meaningful. They carry out their duties to near perfection and with great satisfaction.

On the other hand, there are business and government leaders who see their work flatly as a job. I once had a conversation with a government leader who did not want to spend an extra minute on the job even to go to the on-site gym to get in shape, as he knew he should. He wanted to leave his workplace the very minute the clock struck five. This guy was in a job, not a calling. And when he retires, I suspect that he'll never have anything further to do with that organization, except to take his pension every month.

Engage the Team

Great leaders make it their priority to help followers discover their natural talents and to develop those talents into true strengths and, thus, thrive. This is best begun by not only encouraging personal assessment but also through group assessment, discussion, and understanding. As mentioned previously, the MBTI, DISC, Clifton StrengthsFinder, and other such instruments provide a terrific starting place. The following are several steps leaders can take to engage their teams and draw them toward seeing work as a calling:

+ **Celebrate diversity** and the strength it brings to any team or organization. You will recall from *Strengths-Based Leadership* that while people aren't necessarily balanced across all four key domains, you will want a balanced team — one strong in all four key domains: Strategic Thinking, Influence, Relationship Building, and Execution. Try to balance leaders with colleagues whose strengths can make up for leaders' challenges and encourage everyone to appreciate each other's strengths and to complement each other.

+ **Match people's strengths** to their jobs. Also, allow people to adapt their jobs to their strengths. Forget strict, uncompromising job descriptions and think about job guidelines that can be adapted to the person and the situation. An executive recruiter friend talks about the "bend-don't-break rule" when it comes to leadership (Kirkman, 2012). Love that analogy.

+ **Become a champion** for your direct reports. Richard Boyatzis talks about developing the ideal self. Like the Army recruiting commercial says: "Be all you can be." And, making that happen for people and teams remains the chief domain of great leaders. One of the much-touted strengths of General Electric is how its talent management system has produced so many strong leaders, including a number of corporate CEOs. Indeed, creating future leaders becomes the mark of a great leader.

+ **Set challenging goals** and make them attainable. Research shows that followers like attainable but tough challenges. However, terms like "stretch goals" can be too confusing. Start with reasonable but difficult goals and stick with them. Follow through—celebrate wins, address losses. This kind of goal setting creates a sense of focus, determination, and finally, a strong sense of hope in the future.

+ **Focus on something BIGGER.** Develop a team/organizational mission, vision, values credo, rooted in meaning and purpose. And when you've done that, look beyond your team to something BIGGER, like the company, community, and country. According to research by psychologist and professor Sonja Lyubomirsky and her colleagues, when people stop focusing on themselves, it makes them happier—regardless of whether they started out happy or depressed.

Again, let's turn to the The Positive Leadership Matrix to keep track of where we are:

How of Positivity	Step#1: Get Social	Step #2: Get Strong	Step #3: Get Positive
Who of Positivity: Leaders can influence	**Personal Life:** Family Friends **Professional Life:** Boss Peers Direct Reports Teams **Engage the Team**	**Know Your Strengths** 360s, MBTI, DISC... **Work in or Work-in Strengths** **Job, Career, Calling** **Engage the Team**	

Step 3: Get Positive in Your Activities

Get fit and enjoy a much better life. Getting fit on several levels — physically, mentally, and emotionally — ensures a higher quality of life and helps you enjoy the gifts and endure the strains of life. Just as an in-shape football player can break for daylight, score a touchdown, and savor the crowd's response, he's equally able to take a hard hit and bounce back without injury, either physical or emotional. Let's explore ways to get physically, mentally, and emotionally in shape.

Physical: Get Fit

Recognize that each of the three forms of physical fitness (sleep, diet, and exercise) that follow is very important. That said, the three will be discussed in order of most important first.

+ **Sleep**: We need a minimum of seven to eight hours of sleep a day (kids need even more). Sleep deprivation leads to diminished capacity and at worst, a form of psychosis! Research has determined that sleep deprivation is a powerful form of torture, used in both Korea and Vietnam to "break" prisoners. In fact, getting only four hours of sleep for more than several days can induce severe psychosis. Not only do we suffer psychological damage; sleep-deprived people also actually put on weight because the body feels like it is being assaulted when it doesn't get the rest it needs and then compensates by storing fat in defense to the assault.

Naps can be a tremendous help in getting the sleep you need to be productive and fit. In *Take a Nap! Change Your Life*, Sara Mednick and Mark Ehrman (Workman, 2006) talk about the organizational advantages of strategic napping. As little as a twenty-minute nap can make a huge difference if you are behind on sleep. Companies like Google have "napping pods" and encourage their employees to nap because they will wake up refreshed and far more productive than if they just tried to power through the day without enough sleep. Getting sleep is your number-one priority for developing your physical fitness. Start here.

+ **Diet**: People in psychological "dissonance" (out of tune) often stop taking care of themselves and spiral into poor eating habits, like slugging down carbohydrates, sweets, even alcohol or drugs, as forms of self-medication and self-soothing. They get a rush from any or all of the above stimulants. Even though the rush is often only temporary, it provides escape. A healthy diet will eventually replace those self-medication urges with new patterns and at the same time balance out the system. Unfortunately, about 90% of dieters fall off the wagon. Socialized dieting (such as using systems like Medifast, Weight Watchers, or Jenny Craig) seems to be a good alternative to climbing this mountain on your own.

+ **Exercise**: Walking and other forms of exercise produce positivity-inducing hormones in the body. There is a robust body of research on these results, sometimes called runner's high or the "rush" of exercise. We know that roughly 150 minutes a week of walking, running, or cycling (any aerobic exercise) can stem the tide of cardiovascular failure.

Attaching exercise to daily routine or habit is the ticket to success. In fact, tying any discipline to routine can guarantee more success than any other practice. Further, removing barriers to things you want to do and putting barriers in front of things you don't want to do (activation energy) seems to be the ultimate ticket to doing good things and avoiding bad ones. Some folks work out in the morning and others at night. Whichever system you pick, see how it fits your daily life and keep the habit going — forever!

One BIG note: Sitting for prolonged periods of time can have a devastating effect on health that even exercise will not mitigate. Studies indicate that more than eleven hours of sitting per day increase the rate of death by 40% regardless of other activity (Sifferlin, 2012). So stand up and move around frequently or face the consequences of never moving again!

Fit teams: Leaders who want healthy, productive teams need to make such health intentional and to lead by example:

+ **Sleep:** Encourage rest, get people out of the office at a decent hour, and ask them NOT to respond to emails or texts at all hours of the night. Set boundaries and encourage rest and relaxation. The return on investment is WELL worth it.

+ **Diet:** Americans are overweight. This leads to a host of problems. Again, leaders help teams by setting an example and getting control of their own weight. Joining

Medifast, Weight Watchers, or Jenny Craig (I have no financial stock in any of these companies) as a team has an invaluable impact on overall corporate health by socializing the process. Offering programs for the team and encouraging healthy living and eating can change the team's overall health and well-being.

+ **Exercise:** Take daily walks at work and encourage fitness for your team. Have meetings while on a walk. Sponsor healthful events at the office. Make health and fitness topics of value with the team. Your healthcare premiums will be affected positively, along with the team's productivity and happiness.

Psychological: Get Psyched

Recall the numbers 50-10-40: Happiness is 50% inherited; 10% life circumstance (divorce, death, jobs, etc.); and 40% under our own control. We CAN change how happy we feel. And, researchers have some ideas about how to do that.

+ **Try meditation**: Take just fifteen to twenty minutes a day to become more mindful—i.e., more present in the moment. Many people live in the past and are often sad about what they did or did not do. Others live in the future and often become anxious about the potential of a worst-case scenario. They worry: What if this happens or if this does not happen? Research in the field of meditation has decades of results to demonstrate that simply being in the present—being only concerned with the here and now—can help us overcome either the regrets of the past or fears of an unpredictable future.

To begin the process, just concentrate only on your breathing—breathing in and out—the very essence of "being" here and now. This simple focus on your breathing pattern can start to calm you down and get you positive.

Typically in meditation instruction we're taught to take in a deep slow breath through the nose, expand the diaphragm (belly breathe), hold it for three seconds, and then slowly release through the mouth. If you repeat this over and over for just fifteen to twenty minutes, you will relax and eventually you'll go into a light unconsciousness—it's not really sleep, but you'll be refreshed when you awake. Another powerful technique recommended by Thich Nhat Hanh (Hanh, 1998), a Buddhist monk and author of numerous books on meditation, follows: As you inhale, say to yourself, "I know that I am breathing in" and as you exhale, say to yourself, "I know that I am breathing out." This technique will keep you focused on your breathing.

Don't worry if other ideas pop into your head, especially when you first start meditating. That's completely normal. Stick with the practice—and you will experience fewer and fewer disruptions over time. Such a daily time investment for peace of mind is well worth developing. Best practice calls for doing about twenty minutes of meditation twice a day—once in the morning and once in the afternoon. Note that you may need to practice this for a week or two, but after a while, it will become as natural as eating or drinking—and as accessible when you need it—for example, before a big presentation at work.

+ Practice mindfulness: If at first, meditation seems like it might take a lot of time, you might consider the ancient practice of mindfulness, from the Sanskrit word that means awareness—being present in the moment. Taking breaks throughout the day to focus on the present moment even while you are doing something like showering or walking or eating calms the mind. Most of the bad things we conjure up in our minds never happen, yet we spend so much time contemplating worst-case scenarios. Become more present in the moment and aware and watch this change. It takes almost no time and you can do it anywhere, anytime.

+ **Decrease negativity**: Dispute negative thoughts like a lawyer. When you have a persistent negative thought, such as, "I can't do this," argue against it about how you CAN do this! Or, think back on times when you have overcome your self-doubts and bring them forefront in your mind.

+ **STOP rumination**: When you constantly rehash a bad experience, either with yourself or with others around you, it is NOT good for you or for those listening to you. Repetitive venting—contrary to some earlier thinking by psychologists—is harmful, not helpful. Rather than getting into an infinite negative loop, think of a big red **STOP** sign when you start rehashing that bad experience, or simply say out loud or to yourself: "Stop It!" It is not good to keep venting. So, STOP it now!

+ **Savor good thoughts**: Conversely, reminiscing over and over about past good experiences is powerful medicine. When you rethink past positive experiences, your mind and body literally re-experience them. You get relief from the drag of the day by taking a "mini-vacation" in your mind. Thinking about past trips, songs, vacations, all help you take a pleasant mini-trip, all over again. This technique is especially powerful for older people—it's one big consolation of aging.

+ **Invest in positive activities:** Don't just buy stuff. Instead of buying a gadget, go on a great vacation that you can savor long after the experience. Investing in experiences, not just stuff, takes your positivity much further. Tickets to a play or a holiday with friends will make you feel much better than strutting your stuff—like a new car—in front of others.

+ **Become a "YES" man or woman**: Remember John Gott-man's advice about starting from a positive place? In the *Harvard Business Review* interview, he used the image of a salt shaker. If we want a great relationship with our spouses (or really anyone), he explained, we should envision big salt shaker full of "YESes" and sprinkle those "yeses" over everyone and everything that moves! When your husband or wife asks if you would like to go on a trip, your answer should be YES. And when your kid asks if you'd like to toss a ball back and forth, your response should be YES. Start from YES and see the difference it makes in relationships.

Unfortunately, some people respond to any request with a "NO" that has to be negotiated to a yes. That exercise becomes wearisome over time for others and eventually leads to a toxic or avoidant relationship. Start with YES and see the difference it makes in your life.

+ **Cultivate positive habits**: Research has taught us that will-power alone does not work. As just one simple example, remember how many people fall off of diets (90%). Psychologists have determined that we have a limited fount of willpower. If we spend all day fighting temptation and using up our ration of willpower, it's no wonder we just give up when we go home at night, completely depleted.

On the other hand, using "activation energy" can make a huge big difference in success or failure (Achor, 2010). According to this psychological phenomenon, if you make it easy to do things that are good for you and hard to do things that are bad for you, excellent things happen. For example, put your gym bag close to the front door to remind you to start your day by getting fit! If you start to drink at a bar, give your keys to a "designated driver" to avoid the temptation to drink and drive. If you like ice cream but are putting on weight, avoid the path home at night that takes you past a Baskin Robbins (this is autobiographical!).

Psyched Teams

Leaders set the tone and atmosphere wherein cultures can develop, thrive, and attract great new followers. And great followers make great teams. To keep teams psyched, try the following techniques. I hope they inspire you to come up with many others of your own:

+ **Meditation**: Practice meditation at work and encourage others to do so, especially after lunch. It's amazing how much of an energy boost people get from twenty minutes of quiet meditation after lunch. Note: Meditation is not "sleeping on the job," but a powerful precursor to good work.

+ **Focus on happiness**: Make positivity central to your company. Include it in your values statement. Make it something you consider on your evaluations. Consider it part of what you stand for — the kind of quality you'd hire for and fire for.

+ **Just say yes**: Get the team to practice saying "yes." At first this might prove harder than you might think. But if it becomes part of an intentional culture, before long you'll hear the corporate dialog begin to shift toward positivity.

+ **Stop rumination**: Set up a signal within the team that will be used when a team member begins to over-ruminate about a loss. Sure, raise the issue, discuss it, and take corrective action as a team. But don't let anyone beat that horse to death.

+ **Encourage positivity**: Just as you'll want to stop the highly infectious disease of negative rumination, you will want to spread the equally contagious habit of positivity. Celebrate team wins and savor them over and over. Getting teams to remember how they faced a challenge in the past and how they worked together to overcome it provides a path—a former bright spot to help them face a new challenge.

Practice the "Big Four": Gratitude, Kindness, Optimism (and Hope), and Love

Leaders are not only the moral compasses of organizations, but they are also the Morale Compasses. Leaders create emotion and mood, and eventually they shape culture.

To create a positive and a productive atmosphere, leaders must first get themselves into that mode, and then pass it along—by example. The essence of creating such an atmosphere stems from practicing positive emotions that shift mood and eventually culture. Martin Seligman, Barbara Frederickson, Richard Boyatzis, Ed Diener, Shawn Achor, Tal Ben Sahara, Sonja Lyubomirsky and other scholars note that we have a number of positive emotions that produce a higher level of happiness in people. In fact, Barbara Frederickson's research (at UNC) reveals that positivity emerges from the following ten positive emotions: joy, gratitude, serenity, interest, hope, pride, amusement, inspiration, awe, and love (Fredrickson, 2009). For ease of memory and focus, I've aggregated them into the BIG Four: Gratitude, Kindness, Optimism (and Hope), and Love. What follows are some practical ways to infuse yourself and your team with positive emotions to prepare them to perform at the highest levels, with the least amount of friction.

#1. Gratitude: Simply put, to increase happiness and stave off depression, we all would do well to develop an "attitude of gratitude"—i.e., to make gratitude a way of life. Scientists have developed ways to test this hypothesis with incredible results. For example, Seligman asked severely depressed people to keep a "three blessings" journal or to just list three things "that went well" today in their journal. After only fifteen days of this seemingly benign activity, even these severely depressed people experienced great relief and significant gains in happiness (Seligman, 2012). Simply by writing down three things that went well during the day helps people see things in their daily lives that make life worth living for. Having done this activity for now well over a year, I can personally attest to this simple exercise's effectiveness. I keep a small pocket journal in my medicine cabinet and make my entries every night before flossing and brushing my teeth. Linking this simple but powerful exercise to a long-established daily habit keeps the activity (journal entry) alive and well.

Seligman and others recommend a gratitude visit as a healthy gratitude exercise. This entails writing out what this person did that made you so grateful for them—then going to the person and telling him or her what s/he means to you. Seligman reports that this is one of the most powerful exercises of appreciation and gratitude anyone can perform.

"Thank you" notes or emails also work well to express your gratitude. Over the Christmas and New Year holidays for the past two years, I've started sending thank you notes to my colleagues and clients as well as to my family. Over the course of a few weeks, I write about fifty such notes and get return notes with some of the nicest responses you could imagine—some much nicer than what I had written. The key for me is to keep them personal and specific, and limit them to a short paragraph.

One final note on gratitude: Whatever you note in your journal about gratitude does not have to be anything major. This morning on the way to the coffee shop where I write, for example, I sat at a stop light on a very busy road. As I waited for the light to turn green, I noticed the different sounds of tires on different vehicles, the soft wind hitting a gorgeous fern tree that I'd never before noticed, the glint of early morning light on a street sign, and how lucky I was to be in a state of mindfulness—in that very moment perfectly content with my life. Not a bad way to start a writing session.

Gratitude for teams. Here are a few things you could try with your teams, under the collective banner of "positive priming," which is a key factor in success.

+ Positive priming is what Boyatzis calls "the positive attractor" (Boyatzis &McKee, 2005). Teams (and people) perform better when primed positively first. And Shawn Achor points to a pile of research noted in his book *The Happiness Advantage: The Seven Principles of Positive Psychology That Fuel Success and Performance at Work* (Crown Business, 2010) that confirms Boyatzis' idea.

Here are some examples: Students perform better on standardized tests like the SATs when they are asked to think of something in the past that made them happy prior to taking the test. Doctors diagnose quicker and better when given a piece of candy (and told not to eat it until after the experiment) before making a diagnosis. Athletes perform at maximal levels, accomplishing seemingly impossible feats, when they meditate and envision themselves repeatedly succeeding.

To "positively prime" your team:

+ Start every meeting with a "positive moment." Ask each attendee to cite one good thing going on in his/her department, life, or family.

+ When you sit down to do either a peer review or performance review, use the formula: P-Q-P. First, Praise the person or team. Be specific and enthusiastic. Next, ask Questions around issues or performance of which you're unsure. Finally, Polish—offer suggestions that might make the product or service even better.

+ Ask all team members to write down two to three things they appreciate in each other. Or you can write the items on yellow stickies and put them under each person's name on a board that you've set up for this purpose.

+ End meetings on a high note — name one person in the room for whom you're grateful. Name two things you learned and are grateful for. People take turns ending the meeting (they know ahead of time when it will be their turn).

+ Send a gratitude note to an entire team or to an individual contributor. Be specific and enthusiastic in your praise. If you're willing, go and tell that person face-to-face what you're grateful for — it's powerful stuff.

+ Make up your own gratitude exercises. Ask the team to come up with a few "gratitude gestures." You'll only be limited by your team's imagination.

#2. Kindness: Compassion, empathy, or caring for others — however you describe the act of kindness — is one of my "Big Four" because of its strong effects not only on those who receive our kindness, but also on those who give it. Brain scans of people who receive acts of kindness show that the rewards part of the brain lights up brightly when they receive a gift. Moreover, the same spot in the brain of the giver lights up — only in a bigger, more robust way! So when your mother said, "It's better to give than to receive," she was absolutely correct.

Random acts of kindness are just one of several techniques you might try. Here's an example: On your way to work, allow a fellow commuter to merge into traffic. It's a simple act; however, I've noticed just how powerful and infectious this simple act can be. Having let cars merge into my lane on the highway, I've watched them, in turn, allow someone else do the same — a reciprocity of sorts. Gratitude follows a kind act and creates an atmosphere that predisposes others to such kindness.

Kind Wednesdays! The research points to picking one day a week to be very intentional about your kindness if you want to get the best results. That's not to say that you act like a selfish jerk the rest of the week! Quite the opposite. It presumes you are kind every day, and that one day of the week you get very intentional about doing five special things. I have chosen Wednesdays to perform my acts of kindness. So on Tuesdays, I think about the people for whom I'll do something kind, and what (specifically) I'll do.

Today, as I write this, is actually a Tuesday. And here's what I'll do tomorrow:

1. Write a letter to Oscar (VP of service for the local Honda dealership) and copy his boss about how Oscar helped my daughter.

2. Send flowers to Nycele, our new receptionist.

3. Buy a colleague a cup of coffee at Starbucks.

4. Thank the coffee guys tomorrow and give them a copy of the new book that just came out, which I wrote in the back table at their shop.

5. Be nice to someone in traffic today! Note that the size of the act is not as important as the intentionality of the acts.

Kindness for teams: An act of intentional kindness spreads like a virus—a very good virus. The theory of reciprocity drives this viral response.

We all have felt the pull of "paying back" whatever we receive. On the negative side, that "reciprocity" can be a vengeful, negative force (vicious cycle), but on the more positive side, it makes for a "virtuous cycle," which "lifts all boats" on the team.

+ **Celebrate success**: Cheer when someone hits a goal. Hold them up to the group for praise. We often miss clear and present opportunities to simply celebrate our daily wins— our blessings. We get so caught up in our lives that we are often blind to our own routine successes. So, celebrate success whenever you are able and encourage the team to do the same.

+ **Kind day**: Have the team pick one day of the week for people to be intentionally kind. Ask everyone to "buddy up" and hold each other accountable. An easy way to do this is construct your list the day before your "Kind Day" and send it to a colleague. Ask him or her to do the same and then check in with each other at the end of the week.

#3. Optimism (and hope): Optimism is all about developing a positive mindset about life. In essence, optimism is a joy that can be learned. Much work has been done in this field and again, Martin Seligman stands at the forefront.

Seligman's interest in pessimism led to studies of learned helplessness (the concept that some people just give up when faced with constant adversity that appears unrelenting) and eventually to his concept of learned optimism. According to his research, pessimists accept adversity as just the way things go for them. For pessimists, the locus of control is outside them, thus, they often see themselves as victims, not leading actors in the play of their own lives. Optimists, on the other hand, believe the locus of control resides within themselves and thus view themselves as activists and adversity as an issue to figure out, overcome, and use to move forward. Optimists actually get stronger after adversity, whereas pessimists are traumatized by it. Here's a stark example: Soldiers who are depressed and who are then brutally injured (either physically or psychologically) in war often suffer from what we know as Post-Traumatic Stress Disorder (PTSD). However, soldiers who are optimistic and then experience the same sort of brutal injury actually gain from the experience, a phenomenon called Post-Traumatic Growth (Seligman, 2012).

I first experienced this phenomenon years ago when I visited the Vietnam Memorial. At the time, I was an FBI agent. As I walked along the wall looking for names of fellow Marines who had died in the War, I noticed a number of Vietnam Vets huddled on the periphery, some in tents, others sitting on mats asking for money from memorial visitors. They still wore remnants of their old uniforms — hats, medals, shirts, and field jackets. At that precise moment this thought came to mind, *"What makes those guys so different from me and others who experienced the same horrors of war but took a different path?"* Seligman's research that I read many years later has answered the question for me. The good news: Seligman and his colleagues are now teaching coping techniques to the Army as a way of stemming the suicide rate — which has become an epidemic for vets of the wars in Iraq and Afghanistan.

Learned optimism is one of Seligman's big discoveries. He based this discovery on his work on learned helplessness. Turning the concept on its head, Seligman built on Albert Ellis' ABC model (Adversity-Belief-Consequence) by adding two additional steps: Disputation and Energization. Thus, Seligman's method is called the ABCDE Model. In essence, it involves telling a different "narrative" or story to ourselves when faced with adversity — an optimistic narrative. Here's what it looks like in brief:

1. **A**dversity: My boss just yelled at me in a staff meeting.
2. **B**elief: He's a real jerk!
3. **C**onsequence: I avoid talking to him, and our relationship deteriorates even more.
4. **D**isputation: Maybe he's getting a lot of pressure from corporate and is just over-reacting.
5. **E**nergization: I'm feeling better that there might be a better explanation for his conduct. I'll chat with him when things simmer down.

Hope is closely related to optimism and creates a positive and resilient mindset — important for growth and flourishing (Seligman, 2012). Moreover, Stanford psychologist Carol Dweck's research around the differences between a fixed and a growth mindset (Dweck, 2006) helps us understand both optimism and hope.

Dweck observed that people with a fixed mindset operate from a philosophy that their very basic qualities—such as personality, intelligence, and talents—are immutable. You have what you got and you do the best you can with it. However, people with a growth mindset believe that their basic abilities can change and be augmented with work and determination. These folks like to learn and are resilient in the face of failure. Dweck's research leads her to believe that all great people have a growth mindset.

So consider optimism as the baseline for growth and positivity. However, understand the difference between hope and optimism: While optimism creates a growth and a positive mindset (one that expects the best), hope creates the path toward a goal. Think of hope and optimism as two sides of a coin: optimism is the visionary side, hope is the practical side.

Similarly, consider Rick Snyder's research on hope. He concluded that hope is a combination of agency thinking and pathways thinking. Agency thinking means you believe you are capable of achieving your goal. This can be increased by encouraging people to think about their past successes. Pathways thinking is when you see several ways to achieve your goal. This can be increased by helping people brainstorm ideas for accomplishing their goals (Snyder, 1994).

Boyatzis and McKee in *Resonant Leadership* (Harvard Business Review Press, 2005) explore the importance of hope for leaders who are in tune (resonant) with their followers. Though mindfulness prepares leaders to interact with others, it's not enough to protect themselves from the "dissonance" default. However, hope is a powerful "reset button" for us all. Hope helps leaders focus on their vision for the future. And vision becomes a very powerful "positive attractor" that takes us down a path of renewal and away from dissonance—and from being out of sync with followers.

Boyatzis and McKee cite examples of how positive visioning has helped great athletes win under the most stressful of situations—principally by envisioning themselves winning—with great detail. The neural paths created by such specific and repetitive envisioning are very similar to those who have practiced such skills for a long period of time. As a positive attractor, hope becomes like an umbrella of positive protection that draws from leaders' strengths and visions of a successful future. The result is slower breathing, better memory, and in general a healthier prognosis, whereas negative attractors like hate, jealousy, and envy take leaders down a very different path — one of emotional, physical, and spiritual isolation and dissonance. Not fun. The authors offer several key components of hope. Leaders need to:

1. Have a clear vision for the future of the organization.
2. Be in touch with people around them.
3. Possess an optimistic mindset.
4. See their vision as feasible.

Optimism and hope for teams: Envisioning a better future makes every day more purposeful. Leaders who demonstrate optimism daily provide hope in the future. Time and again both optimism and hope — a paired couple — float to the surface of research as being qualities of leaders whom others want to follow. By setting a hopeful vision for the team, leaders can create a clear, powerful path forward. A leader's optimistic (and realistic) vision helps structure a hopeful path toward the future. And a hopeful path is one most likely to be taken and completed.

#4. Love: In the late 1930s, the most extensive longitudinal study ever conducted began. Tracing the physical, mental, and social health of 268 sophomores at Harvard and funded by the William T. Grant Foundation, this study revealed powerful insights into adult development and aging.

Psychiatrist George Vaillant took over the reins of this study when he was only thirty-three, tracking this group of men (Harvard was only male back then) well into their eighties. Himself now an elder, Vaillant has written his magnum opus, *Triumphs of Experience: The Men of the Harvard Grant Study* (Belknap Press, 2012). An accessible and detailed account of the Grant study, written by Joshua Wolf Shenk and published in the *Atlantic Monthly*, details the study's key insights. The following comments summarize points made by Shenk in his engaging piece, "What Makes Us Happy" (Shenk, 2009).

If Vaillant's exhaustive study proved anything, it was that men who were in loving, intimate relationships lived longer and were happier. Moreover, as he traced these men from youthful undergrads to old age, Vaillant's lens was focused not on seeing how successful the men were but on how they dealt with adversity and how adaptation morphed their lives. He observed the subjects' defense mechanisms, "…unconscious thoughts and behaviors that you could say either shape or distort—depending on whether you approve or disapprove—a person's reality" (Shenk, 2009).

Defense mechanisms are the psychological equivalent of first aid. When we experience a deep psychological wound, our brains rush in to apply a bandage to protect ourselves. Vaillant offers a hierarchy of defensive responses from the unhealthiest to the healthiest. At the bottom of this hierarchy are those he calls unhealthy psychotic defense mechanisms to help us deal with stress. Such responses as hallucination or paranoia may help some people adapt; however, they make us appear imbalanced and disturbed to others around us. At the next level are "immature" defense mechanisms like passive aggressiveness, hypochondria, and projection, which do not make us look deranged but do hamper intimacy with others around us. The next level toward normalcy— "neurotic" adaptive defense mechanisms— include intellection, dissociation, and repression. Finally, "mature responses" to stress include altruism, humor, and suppression. People with these types of responses are the most lovable, those most likely to adapt and thrive in life, especially as they age. To underscore a previous comment--men (the primary subjects of this study) who were in loving, intimate relationships lived longer and were happier.

In related work concerning positivity and happiness, a whole specialty of psychology has emerged called positive psychology. University of North Carolina's Barbara Frederickson wrote a number of publications on this topic, including her bestseller *Positivity*. Frederickson has just authored a new book, *Love 2.0: How Our Supreme Emotion Affects Everything We Feel, Think, Do, and Become* (Hudson Street Press, 2013). In this book, she asks us to suspend our most common thoughts of what love is, namely, sex, commitment, exclusive, unconditional, and lasting. Rather, she defines love as "...an emotion, a momentary state that arises to infuse your mind and body alike." Based on Frederickson's research, love is available to us all the time, not just when we're with our spouses, partners, or other "loved ones":

> ...Love is the momentary upwelling of three tightly interwoven events: First, a sharing of one or more positive emotions (joy, gratitude, hope...) between you and another; second, a synchrony between your and the other person's biochemistry and behaviors; and third, a reflected motive to invest in each other's well-being that brings mutual care" (Frederickson, 2013).

Thus, in every strongly personal interaction, we are falling in love, in a way that's momentary, positive, and mind altering.

Frederickson calls love a "micro-moment of positivity resonance" that can be experienced between any two people, anytime, anywhere. "Love is our supreme emotion: Its presence or absence in our lives influences everything we feel, think, do and become" (Fredrickson, 2013, p. 14). And while we can think of people we love and get a positive kick or boost from that image, love will only work when we are with another person. This "love connection" happens within a biological system involving mirror neurons, oxytocin, and vagal tone. Here's a summary of what Frederickson has to say about these three.

1. Mirror neurons are those neurons in each of us that mimic the actions and brain waves of another when we "synch up" with that person. Italian scientists discovered this phenomenon when studying monkeys whose brain activity they were tracking. The scientists noted that when, on a hot day, a scientist lifted an ice cream cone to his mouth,

the brain of an experimental monkey was stimulated. Specifically, the neurons that controlled the monkey's arm, the one that mirrored the arm of the scientist lifting the cone to his lips, were stimulated, as if the monkey itself were eating the cone! The old adage "monkey see, monkey do" has real scientific basis. Conclusion? The more synchronous people act in each other's presence, the more loving toward each other they become; one action of love stimulates another action of love in return.

2. Oxytocin (affectionately called the "cuddle hormone") is given off every time two people connect intimately. This could be when two friends meet and hug, when a parent plays directly with a child on the floor, when two business colleagues are involved in a meaningful and safe conversation. In essence, oxytocin (which stimulates trust and openness) is the opposite of epinephrine or cortisol (which stimulates fear and distrust).

3. "Vagal tone" is the final component in these loving "micro-moments of positivity resonance." One of the brain's cranial nerves, the vagus nerve, connects heart to head… it controls the rate at which your heart beats and therefore your blood pressure and your breathing. This nerve stimulates your eyes and facial muscles and makes it easier for you to mirror another person's expressions. Thus, we smile when a friend smiles and look sad as they tell us a sad story about their life.

"Vagal tone" is the association between heart rate and breathing. People with high vagal tone are able to control their emotions and are far more socially adept than others at friendships, love, and connection. Interestingly, you don't have to be born with this capacity for vagal tone; you can meditate your way into it. Experiments by Frederickson on the Buddhist practice of loving-kindness meditation have proven that people who use this type of meditation increased their vagal tone and thus their capacity for love (they were more prone to loving moments in their lives) and for a healthier life. Such increased vagal tone lowered their susceptibility to debilitating diseases like heart disease and diabetes.

The bottom line: If you're searching for the ONE true love of your life, you may be disappointed and become lonely. And, isolation is the absolute killer to love! However, it you accept that love can come in micro-moments a number of times a day at work, at home, and just out in the community, you're more likely to experience love at home, at work, and at play. Those micro-moments put your body and mind in a very positive place...and make you more open to finding a mate or a lifelong friend.

+ People can practice love by doing things together. The array is limitless:

+ Telling stories

+ Singing

+ Running and cycling together

+ Taking a walk together and talking

+ Dancing

+ Any of an endless number of interconnected experiences...where a chance for a micro-moment of positivity resonance exists.

Love for teams: When we discuss love and teams, it's closer to shared micro-moments of positive resonance. So, when team members get lunch together, tell jokes to each other, and share hopes and dreams, they are experiencing a form of love. That is to say that among strong teams, there is a bond of caring that goes beyond merely what the person can do for the team. It's more about caring for the person, the person's work, and the person's family. What most often separates low- from high-performing teams is the degree to which caring and love become part of the team's core DNA. Celebrating birthdays, graduations, and births, as well as mourning deaths, losses, and even failures, helps teams act and think like loving families. Such strong ties produce more engagement and ultimately greater profits, success, and genuine happiness.

Let's again turn to The Positive Leadership Matrix to keep track of where we are:

How of Positivity	Step #1: Get Social	Step #2: Get Strong	Step #3: Get Positive
Who of Positivity: Leaders Can Influence	**Personal Life:** Family Friends **Professional Life:** Boss Peers Direct Reports Teams	**Know Your Strengths** MBTI DISC StrengthsFinder Values in Action **Work in or Work-in Strengths** **Elevate Your Work** -Job -Career -Calling	**Get Fit** Sleep and Diet Meditation Physical Fitness **Get Psyched** Stop Neg. Thoughts Savor Pos. Thoughts Say "Yes" **Practice the BIG Four:** G, K, O&H, L Gratitude, Kindness, Optimism (and Hope), and Love.

Key Points to Remember

To embrace Positive Leadership, leaders must become intentional. Positivity and happiness lie well within our control. Remember Sonya Lyubomirsky's 50-10-40 equation: 50% of our happiness is inherited (it's in the specific genetic cards we're dealt); 10% is the result of all our life experiences combined (but no more, even for the toughest of lives); and 40% comes from what we do intentionally to have a better, happier, more positive life. That's a huge percentage under our personal control!

What's more, leaders,have great influence in creating high-performing followers and teams—both of which determine whether companies succeed or fail. Research demonstrates that positive leaders make a significant difference on the level of employee engagement, which leads to productivity differences of up to 20%. Unfortunately, 80% of workers today are unengaged. That lack of productivity is a staggering 24% deficit when calculated for companies with revenues of all sizes, from $100,000 to $1 billion or more a year. However, leaders can directly affect the level of followers' positivity, engagement, and productivity. Thus, positive leadership presents a powerful return on investment that organizations ought to take seriously.

A scan of the most important research in positive psychology reveals several compelling paths toward positivity and happiness for leaders:

1. **Get social in your relationships**. There is no stronger single determiner of happiness than the strength and depth of your social networks. Developing intentional, lasting, and strong social networks with family, friends, and co-workers (bosses, peers, and direct reports) provides the best positivity and happiness insurance policy you can purchase. Teams present a particular social advantage to companies. Learning how to communicate with, motivate, and treat teams as important groups of key people remains both a challenge and opportunity for any leader.

2. **Get strong at work**. You spend most of your waking hours at work. One could easily argue that you spend more "alert" time with co-workers than with family members. Spending such quality time with people and work that you love can make a huge difference in your happiness and positivity levels. Thus, understanding your particular and personal strengths by using one of a number of instruments (MBTI, DISC, and StrengthsFinder), will give insight into various types of personalities, preferences, and jobs that will likely yield happiness and productivity in your life. Even when your job responsibilities and critical elements are not perfectly suited to your preferences, you can "work in" your strengths by volunteering to be on interdepartmental teams or taking on extra assignments at work, and even volunteering for nonprofit organizations outside of work—all to exercise your preferred strengths and feel more fulfilled.

3. **Get positive in your activities**. We all have the opportunity every day to choose to be positive and happy:

   a. *Getting healthy* by meditating (only 15 –20 minutes a day), getting physically fit (150 minutes a week), dieting (watch the calorie count), and good sleep patterns (7–9 hours a night).

   b. *Getting psyched* by stopping rumination of negative thoughts, savoring good experiences over and over again, and starting conversations from a "yes" or "let's-give-it-a-try" predisposition—all of which lead to a positive mindset.

   c. *Practicing positive emotions,* especially the "Big Four": gratitude, kindness, optimism (and hope), and love. Putting on your "BIG Four Positivity Glasses" can help you singlehandedly raise your personal positivity and the way you filter the world. For example, *Gratitude* for even the small, daily gifts (sunrise, health, friend, pets…) can make you much happier within three weeks. *Kindness* —both random and intentional —toward others also raises your own level of happiness. Indeed, acts of kindness create a more powerful psychological "hit" for the giver of kindness than the recipient. *Optimism* (and *Hope*) provides a positive vision of the future and a thoughtful (hopeful) strategy to get there. *Love*, the most powerful emotion of all, gives us the ability to shape our happiness with family, friends, coworkers, and teams.

After a year's worth of researching the researchers and having written out this chapter of my findings, I read *Happiness: Unlocking the Mysteries of Psychological Wealth*, written by Ed Diener and his son Robert Biswas-Diener. I felt amazed and validated when I read their elegant recipe for happiness:

"A life full of love — with others, friends, and colleagues; with work, being engaged in what you love to do every day; and, with experiences, activities, and life in general."

I want to end this section with a short story about an elderly Cherokee chief teaching his grandson about life:

"A fight is going on inside me," he said to the boy. "It is a terrible fight between two wolves.

"One is evil — he is anger, envy, sorrow, regret, greed, arrogance, self-pity, guilt, resentment, inferiority, lies, false pride, superiority, self-doubt, and ego.

"The other is good — he is joy, peace, love, hope, serenity, humility kindness, benevolence, empathy, generosity, truth, compassion, and faith.

"This is the same fight that is going on inside you — and inside every person, too."

The grandson thought about it for a minute and then asked his grandfather, "Grandfather, which wolf will win?"

The old chief simply replied, "The one you feed, my son."

THANK YOU for reading this book. And have a positively great life!

Part II (The Story)–Positive Leadership: The Game Changer at Work

Chapter 1: On the Street

In late December, slumped and gaunt, Jerome Langer sat at his usual place on a short brick wall in front of the chrome-and-steel Metropolitan Office Building. His matted, graying hair stuck out beneath his black woolen hat and his beard made him look like the old man in the sea—much older than his fifty years. Since winter had already set in, he required five layers of clothing from the mission thrift store to stay warm—one more layer than when he first set out to the streets ten months earlier. That, and a bit more wine every month to help stave off the chilling demons.

Today, snowflakes floated down and landed on the olive drab, wool army blanket that covered his head, shoulders, and thinning upper body. With his pale white face peering out from beneath his green cowl, he looked like a tall, thin, ascetic monk. Out of place in this city, where all around him people scurried from cabs into their shiny office buildings, rising hundreds of feet into the cold, gray sky.

Jerome had hit the streets after separating from his wife, Sarah, then losing his public relations job and their home in the suburbs. Now, he sat next to his tin water bucket, which he'd found at the thrift store and bought for a dollar. The gray-pitted bucket had a large handle for hauling. With the bucket and his heavy, dark-green rucksack, he managed to carry all his worldly possessions with him.

Soon one of his regulars—she reminded him of his wife—passed by and tossed a dollar bill into the bucket. "Hey, Jerome. Stay warm."

"Thank you," he responded, working up a smile. Others, refusing to look in his direction, hurried past Jerome to their offices, well above the smells and sounds of the streets below.

Then there was the new CEO, "the Jerk," Jerome called him. When he arrived each morning in his long black limousine and saw panhandlers, he called the cops to roust them all, especially

Jerome, who had staked his claim in front of the Metropolitan building. But Jerome had adapted quickly to this new hassle in his life. Minutes before the Jerk was due to arrive, Jerome always took his bucket and rucksack and ducked behind the bushes on the corner.

However, in February things changed. First, the black limo stopped coming to the building. Then, one day in March, Jerome spotted the Jerk walking into and from the building—again, no limo in sight. Jerome speculated to himself that Mister High-and-Mighty had lost the limo perk when the board of directors decided to cut back on expenses, an imagined narrative that Jerome was more than pleased to tell himself.

Spring weather arrived early that year. The daily police rousting had long since stopped. Life was as good as it got for Jerome these days, though he required increasing doses of wine to sooth his sadness—especially the loss of his wife and his former life.

And that's when things started getting strange.

One Friday in early April, Jerome got ready to slip around the corner as usual to the convenience store for coffee and to buy more wine. He asked Marguerite—his street buddy—to keep an eye on his bucket. Marguerite was a number of years younger than he, an African American, nearly six feet tall herself. She wore long dreadlocks and would have been stunning had she not been so covered in grit and bruised by the wear and tear of the streets. Careful not to intrude on Jerome's territory, Marguerite sometimes worked the other end of the street and had far more wanderlust than Jerome, who fiercely protected his space and bucket.

When he returned to his spot, Jerome found a note rolled around a $100 bill, bounded by an elastic band. The note read: "Love your neighbor as yourself."

"Who dropped this?" he asked Marguerite, showing her the note and the bill.

"Damn, that's a hundred dollar bill."

"Yeah, you see who left it?"

"Nope."

"Sure?"

"What, do I stutter?"

He shrugged off her wise-crack remark. But the more wine he drank and the more he thought about it, the more curious he got. So, he started his own investigation. Each day, for the following week, he motioned to Marguerite to watch his bucket. When she nodded and gestured back, sometimes more inappropriately than others, he headed toward the convenience store, as usual. However, after getting his provisions for the day, he circled back around to the opposite end of the street to observe his bucket and Marguerite. The following Friday, Jerome noticed a well-dressed woman emerge from the Metropolitan building. She walked over to Marguerite and handed her two small packages. Marguerite nodded, put one package into her own coat pocket and tossed the other into Jerome's bucket.

When Jerome returned and found the note and the $100 in the bucket, he asked Marguerite, "What's the deal?"

"Deal?"

"Second week in a row I get money when I go for coffee."

"Coffee, right!" She paused, looking down at the bottle bulge in his right coat pocket.

"Look, I saw the woman give you something."

"What woman? You sure that 'grape' coffee you drinking ain't messed up your head?"

"Stop it. I doubled back on 18th Street. Watched the whole damn thing."

Marguerite smiled for a second, but quickly put on her game face again.

"Look, I got confidences."

"Like you're some kind of priest?"

"Let it go, man."

"Tell me what's going on," he said, staring at her.

"Can't. I promised."

"We've been friends now over five months."

"OK, but all I'm saying is she works on the 30th floor."

"Mahogany row? Where the Jerk is?"

"Yep. It's all I know. The lobby guard told me one day."

"What's her name?"

"Janet's all I know."

The following week, Jerome was returning from his regular trip to the convenience store when he spotted Marguerite talking to Janet. But it was more like they were arguing. Marguerite pointed to the bucket, shrugged her shoulders, and held out her palms as if to say, "I had to tell him." Jerome could tell that Janet was not happy with the conversation. She took back the two packages from Marguerite and returned to her office building.

The following week, this time on a Thursday, Jerome found a new package and another note, which he unfolded. Along with the usual quote it said, "Jerome, please come up to the 30th floor tomorrow at 11:30. – Janet Gergen."

He decided not to tell Marguerite. But the next morning he circled the block around break time, entered the building through the side door, and went directly toward the elevators. The guard just nodded; he didn't say a word. Jerome took the elevator to the 30th floor. There he was greeted by Janet and taken into an office with a corporate name plate that boldly announced the firm's name: Summers Consulting, Inc. Janet asked him to wait in the plush reception area.

Moments later she returned and buzzed open a door into the largest office he'd ever seen. With tall glass windows on two walls that joined in a ninety-degree angle, the massive office overlooked the city and was appointed in crystal lamps, Oriental rugs, and mahogany furniture. The office belonged on a movie set. Sitting in a large leather wing chair facing the cityscape, a tall, white-haired man about Jerome's age, dressed in a blue pin-striped suit, the Jerk, waited. Looking tired and worn, he gestured toward Jerome. "Please," he said pointing toward the matching leather couch.

Jerome smoothed his tattered coat and took off his dark woolen hat, then sat down.

"Look, I have to apologize," the Jerk said.

"Huh?"

"First off, Jerome, I'm Paul Summers," he said. "I'm not sure where to start." He looked out the huge glass window that overlooked the rest of his 18th and K Street palace. "I've, ah…we've. That is, my wife and I… ." He stopped to restart. "About four months ago, my wife and I lost our son, Jake," he said.

Jerome said nothing.

"At the university, he got into drugs."

Jerome listened, resolved to keep quiet.

"He quit school. In and out of rehab."

Jerome nodded slightly.

"I cut him off. Nearly drove my wife crazy." Paul's voice trailed off, but then regained some energy. "We lost contact with him."

Jerome watched as the CEO swallowed and bit his lower lip.

"On December 23rd we got a call from the Boston Police," he said, his voice cracking. "They found Jake in Boston Commons… dead." He battled back tears with so much energy that he shook trying to contain his grief.

"Jake died two days before Christmas. Hypothermia," he said while tears streamed down his face. "He froze to death." He brushed back the tears, cleared his throat, and took a drink of water. "My wife and I separated. I almost quit my job. Instead, I started going to therapy to deal with the pain."

Jerome nodded.

"Those people have helped me deal with my guilt and shame. Suggested I start forgiving myself and make amends with others I've hurt." He paused, looking directly at Jerome. "So I started with you."

Jerome just sat there.

"I've been a jerk. Just wanted to make it up to you somehow — anonymously. But when you figured it out, I thought I owed you an explanation," he said.

Jerome nodded and said, "OK."

"Sorry for all the secrecy, but anonymity helps heal the soul, they told me," the CEO said extending, his hand, which Jerome shook, now ashamed he had not washed up in the restroom on the ground floor before the meeting.

"Thanks," Jerome said. Then he stood and started for the door when the CEO intercepted him and said, "One last thing, Jerome. We're encouraged to take active, positive steps in other people's lives, as well as our own."

"OK," Jerome said.

"So I've taken the liberty to —." He stopped short and then continued, "I'd like you to meet someone I've invited to join us today. Someone very special to you, I believe."

"Who?"

The CEO buzzed Janet and told her to send the guest in. The door opened, and in walked Sarah, Jerome Langer's wife.

Chapter 2: The Reunion

At age forty-seven, Sarah Langer's looks belied her years. She stood about five feet seven but her ramrod-straight posture—an intimidation technique she'd learned practicing corporate law—and her heels made her look much taller. She entered the room with her black long wavy hair pushed back over her camel-haired blazer. Once she got within eyesight of Jerome she stopped dead in her tracks. Looking quickly from him to Paul, she then said, "Paul, what's this all about? You told me you had a legal matter. I..."

"Sarah, please just take a seat, and I'll explain."

Sarah took a seat on the couch across from Jerome, but stared—actually glared—past him with her pale blue eyes riveted on her client, Paul Summers.

Jerome sat there both stunned and angry, though he concealed it, as was his way with Sarah.

Paul read their emotions. "Look, I realize I have no right to meddle into anyone's business..."

"That's right," said Jerome. He started to get up to leave the room.

"Wait, Jerome, just give me a minute here. Please."

Jerome sat back down and stared at the floor as if to say *I'll stay but that's as much as you'll get from me.*

"I had an investigator do a background on you...."

Jerome gave Paul such a look of surprise and distaste that Paul put up his hands as if to say, *Whoa big fella...slow it down.*

"Look, I wanted to figure out how to help. That's when I discovered that Sarah was a corporate attorney. In fact, I'd found out that she was pretty damned good. But I confess I hired her to set up this meeting with you."

Now Sarah looked stunned and angry. "Hired me to set up a meeting. That's what you're saying?"

"It started that way, but I can assure you that our legal counsel has come to rely on your work," Paul said.

"Ridiculous and insulting." She folded her arms.

"Look, just hear me out," he said. "I know that you both separated five months after your daughter was killed in a car accident. Believe me, I know the pain associated with the loss of a child."

Sarah, who had remained stoic until the mention of her daughter, Mary Alice, dabbed the corners of her eyes with a Kleenex.

"When Ellen and I lost our son Jake, I lost my will to even get out of bed. We couldn't talk to each other — unless absolutely necessary. Our marriage tumbled into a free fall. At times I had to remind myself to breathe."

"Look, Paul, I know you think what you're doing is an act of kindness, and I appreciate that," Sarah said. "But Jerome and I are separated. I'm filing for divorce as soon as our one-year separation is up."

Jerome just sat there staring at his feet.

"I get that," Paul said, "but as part of my therapy, I'm trying to work with families who've lost children."

"So now we're part of your therapy! How convenient," Sarah said, with a contemptuous look that could freeze water.

Undeterred, Paul described what had happened to him and his wife. When Jake died, Paul had refused to go to therapy to help him and Ellen discuss and deal with their profound loss. Eventually, Ellen gave him an ultimatum — either get therapy or get out. Paul chose to exit the relationship. His life became extremely difficult, until he met J.C. Williams — an executive coach a friend had used to help get his business back on track. And because Paul had let the consulting business languish, he welcomed talking to J.C. — to do anything that would take his mind off his daughter and marriage.

Finally, Jerome lifted his head and looked first at Sarah, then fixed his gaze on Paul. "So, what does all this have to do with me...us?"

"I want to make you an offer."

Both Sarah and Jerome looked at Paul, but it was Jerome who spoke. "An offer?"

Paul explained that he'd done some research on Jerome's background in public relations — that before his daughter's death, Jerome had been one of the best PR guys in town. Sure, he'd been off the track for almost a year and had deteriorated physically, but Paul could use some staffing augmentation in his marketing/public relations department. Nothing permanent...just a chance to get back on the horse, so to speak. Did Jerome want to give it a try? Paul described the terms: A trial salary about one-half of what the job was worth — with the understanding that if it worked out, the salary would be fully loaded after six months of excellent performance. Then they'd go from there....wherever that led.

"Are you nuts?" said Jerome.

"I've been accused of worse," Paul said, and smiled. It was his first smile of the day.

At that even Jerome cracked a millisecond of a smile — then his face went back to being somber.

"Look, all I'm offering you is a six-month trial at half-pay," Paul said. "As an entrepreneur that's a small bet on a potential big payoff. But there are two conditions."

"Which are?" Jerome asked.

"First, you have to be coached by J.C. Williams for that six months....otherwise no deal."

Jerome again started to get up from the couch when Paul said, "I don't want an answer before you meet with J.C. tomorrow."

"And the second is for you, Sarah. I'm asking you to hold off filing for divorce for six months."

"Absolutely not!"

Paul explained that he knew these requests were equally un-appealing to them both. Then he told them a little bit more about what he knew--that prior to their separation, they had agreed to letting their daughter's friends set up a donor-advised fund at the local Community Foundation to fund a safe driving campaign at the high school — in Mary Alice's name.

Paul cleared his throat. "Look I know that each of you wants to do something to stop kids from texting and driving," he said. "I read the appeal that you both issued in the paper when you announced the fund."

"You're meddling in our lives," Jerome said, then looked at Sarah, who was staring at her watch.

"With a purpose...I admit. If you both take me up on my two conditions — coaching for you, Jerome, and holding off for six months to file for divorce for you, Sarah, I will personally make a $100,000 donation to Mary Alice's fund to stop teenage texting while driving. How's that sound?"

"Crazy," Jerome blurted out uncharacteristically.

"I don't know," Sarah said, looking at Jerome.

"This makes no sense....I, ah," Jerome stuttered.

"Look, just meet with J.C. tomorrow. If you don't like him, deal's off, and you go back to the street. OK?" Paul asked looking directly at Jerome.

Jerome sat for what seemed a long time, slowly nodded a re-luctant "yes," and then rose to his feet. He seemed taller, Sarah thought, as he tossed back his graying, matted hair.

"Sarah, how about you?" Paul asked.

"Not sure."

"Fair enough. How about we wait a week or so and see how things proceed. Can we at least agree not to agree to anything, yet?"

Both of them nodded "yes," however reluctantly.

"Thank you both for coming today," Paul said.

Chapter 3: The Meetings

A few weeks passed — a couple of meetings, some tears, and finally a trial agreement to test out Paul's proposition.

Jerome's first day on the job felt somewhat like an emotional rollercoaster. He'd spent much of the week cleaning up, moving into a Goodwill shelter, getting some second-hand clothes from the store attached to the shelter, and getting his hair cut and beard trimmed.

Janet had given him a list of orientation meetings his first day, and armed with that list he headed for Rachel Szabo's office like a nervous new kid entering high school. Rachel, the senior vice-president of marketing, communications, and public relations, thought Jerome looked exactly like a college professor she'd had in graduate school. Rachel was a large woman — tall and thick — with salt and pepper curly dark hair. She'd been with the company since grad school, twenty-five years ago, when she met Paul, who was then starting up his consulting firm. He'd made her an equity partner fifteen years ago, when she'd turned forty, to keep her — she was extremely smart.

"So, you're the homeless guy! You clean up well," Rachel said, pointing to a chair in front of her large and cluttered desk. "Have a seat."

Jerome's visceral reaction was to leave — now. But he fought against his instinct and sat.

"OK," she said putting down her pen and hiking her reading glasses into her thick hair. "Paul takes on strays all the time. Saving the world, one starfish at a time."

"Excuse me?" Jerome said.

"It's an old parable. Anyway. I'm supposed to train you, get you back into the flow of business. Frankly, I'm too busy to hold your hand. I need help, not a social rehab project."

"I don't want to be a rehab project...or be here...for that matter."

"Sounds good to me. Then, good luck." She stood up and was about to initiate a handshake but thought better of it and refrained.

Jerome got up and walked out. He took off his sport coat, loosened his tie, and decided to head back to the shelter. But Janet caught him and told him that J.C. was in the conference room waiting to meet with Jerome. Exasperated, Jerome nodded. He stopped into the bathroom to collect himself, adjust his tie, and put the coat back on. He'd do this interview and then leave.

J.C. Williams was standing and looking out the window when Jerome entered the room. About the same height as Jerome, with sandy long hair, pale-blue eyes, and an infectious smile, he stuck out his hand and said, "Hey, I'm J.C. Williams."

"Jerome. Jerome Langer."

"Pretty cool view," J.C. said, pointing toward the large glass windows that just happened to look down to the wall where Jerome used to perch.

"Yes…guess so."

Jerome had looked up J.C. on the Internet. At forty-two years old, J.C. had become one of the region's and perhaps the country's best-known executive coaches. A former Rhodes Scholar, he had graduated from Harvard as an undergrad, then Stanford's Business School for both his MBA and doctorate. After graduation, he taught at Darden and quickly became one of the most popular (and youngest tenured) professors there—teaching leadership and organization development. Then he contracted cancer—oddly, a relatively rare and virulent form of breast cancer—and left teaching to eventually become an executive coach in the Washington Metro area.

"Paul tells me you had a great career in public relations. You want to tell me a little about that part of your life?"

"OK…I guess." Jerome stumbled into a recitation of his work experience that felt like he was telling someone else's story. He'd finished graduate school with a master of fine arts degree in writing. Ultimately, he had wanted to become a novelist and despite critical acclaim for his senior novella project — *The Final Temptation* — had to take a copywriting job at Warner PR Associates, a small firm in DC, which struck the mother lode when a certain Virginia senator used them to capture a hotly contested senate seat. It was Jerome's stump speech — The Diversity Quilt — that had proven to be a tipping point for the senator.

The speech outlined how the uniquely diverse quilts his grandmother used to sew for each of her grandchildren — different colors, different sizes, different weaves and fabrics, varied patterns, and one thread piecing each one together to make a unified, beautiful work of art — had become the way he thought of America. At the end of the speech, the senator pulled out the baby quilt Jerome had supplied for him and asked all Americans to add to it. It was corny, schmaltzy, even hokey — and wildly successful. It not only launched the senator but Jerome into the limelight. The rest was a hockey-stick graph of success.

Jerome worked for the senator for six years — long enough to get him re-elected. Then, on to a couple of PR firms, where he did increasingly well — both professionally and financially. Finally he started his own firm and began re-writing his novella into a full-fledged novel. At the top of his career, Mary Alice was killed — as was his desire to press on with anything, including his marriage. When he finished his recitation, Jerome was spent.

"Thank you for sharing the details of your life with me. I know that's not easy to do, especially with a total stranger," J.C. said. "I appreciate the trust and will hope to live up to it as we chat."

Jerome nodded slightly.

"I'm guessing that by now you've already checked me out on the Internet?"

Again, Jerome nodded.

"So, I'm not going to bore you with my story, only to tell you that leadership and coaching have become my passions because

I've watched good leaders and bad leaders and the incredible difference they make in people's lives."

Over the course of the hour, J.C. asked Jerome a number of questions and Jerome asked several himself—mostly around the nature of the coaching process.

J.C. explained that coaching was about asking questions that allowed clients to solve their own issues. Unlike consulting where experts gave advice, executive coaches asked their clients great questions. The steps were easy…identify the Issue, assess the Impact, craft a vision of the Ideal state, and then ask for Intention going forward. J.C. called it The Four I's.

"Hmm," Jerome said.

"Want to try it out to see how it works?" J.C. asked.

"OK."

"So, what's the biggest issue you're facing today…right now?"

Jerome thought for about thirty seconds and said, "Rachel Szabo."

J.C. laughed. "You too?"

"What?"

"You're not the first person to ever identify Rachel as, well, an….issue."

Jerome allowed himself a brief smile.

"So, exactly how does Rachel come across to you?"

"Brash, insensitive, and self-absorbed."

"Well, I'd say you're a pretty good quick study," J.C. smiled.

J.C. asked and Jerome answered a number of questions about the Issue—Rachel. What about her annoyed Jerome so much? What had their first encounter been like? Had Jerome ever had this kind of reaction before to a boss? And so on.

They discussed the Impact of Jerome's visceral dislike of his proposed new boss. Needless to say, the impact was intense enough to have him heading straight for the door — before Janet redirected him to meet with J.C.

"OK...I get how you feel about Rachel today. Understandable. But what if a magic wand hit and tomorrow when you walked in she were your Ideal boss. What might that look like?"

"Magic...ideal? Hmm. Well, I guess we'd get a cup of coffee. Start off slow, kind of like you did. Get to know each other. Stay open to possibilities...that sort of thing."

"OK. Good. So, it would be informal, chatty, over coffee, start slow....that kind of thing?"

"Yep, I'd say so."

They chatted about how the relationship could move forward, given Rachel's insatiable need for recognition and dominance. And by the end of this part of the discussion, Jerome had a long list of potential steps to develop his relationship toward this ideal as much as possible.

"Great," said J.C., "let's move on to Intention. What's one simple step you might take in your journey? Remember the journey of a thousand miles...."

"Starts with the first step — I used Lao Tzu's quote in the senator's speech all the time."

"Exactly...so what is the first step you can take?"

"I guess, showing up again tomorrow?"

"Bingo! Sounds like one small step for man...."

"A big step for mankind!" Jerome said, quoting what astronaut Neil Armstrong had said when he first set foot on the moon in 1969.

"We've got to stop finishing each other's sentences!" J.C. said. He stood up, walked from behind the desk, and shook Jerome's hand with a real man-shake.

The last meeting that morning—before lunch with Paul—was with Sam Wood, the tech guy for the company.

At about 250 pounds, thick as a block of granite but not muscular, Sam Wood, an African American, stood about six feet tall but was about four feet wide. His thick dark curly black hair was pulled back tightly, unlike his beard, which was out there and free, much like Sam's personality. But the first things anyone noticed about Sam were his broad, white-toothy smile and his loud barrel-belly laugh. In fact, you more often heard Sam before you actually saw him.

And so it was that day when Jerome first met Sam.

As Jerome rounded the corner to walk into Sam's office, he heard a deep-voiced bellow issue forth—"HA, HA...NOW that is funny!"—from an office absolutely cluttered with every gadget you could imagine. Old routers; laptops of every era and make—HPs, Dells and Macs; four huge monitors up and running with data...two Mac 36-inchers side by side and two Dells on the other side of his desk. On one wall were pictures of Mr. Spock, Captain Kirk, and the entire Enterprise Crew and on the other were Yoda, Hans Solo, and Chewie, along with Luke and Darth Vadar. Then stacks of tech STUFF in piles of indiscernible organization—indiscernible except to Sam. It looked like a hoarder had met a Trekkie and given birth to Tech Transformer.

When Jerome rounded the corner to enter the office, he stopped short, narrowly missing stepping on a digital recorder on the floor about a foot into the Star Chamber!

Still on the phone with someone, Sam smiled a toothy grin and pointed to a chair half full of stuff pushed to the side for Jerome to sit. Jerome accommodated himself to the space by gently moving things to the side of the seat.

"Well, Jack. I gotta run...you stay dry and tight, my friend!" Sam said. He hung up the phone and then stood and reached his massive hand across the cluttered desk.

"You must be Jerome."

"Yes, hello, and you must be Sam."

"All day long...HA-HA!" Sam guffawed as he was accustomed to in response to his own jokes. As his girlfriend Carol always said, Sam was his own best audience.

Jerome smiled slightly.

Sam looked at Jerome as if he were going to fit him for a new suit and said, "Let me guess Mac or PC, let's see." He stroked an imaginary beard. "You look like a Mac guy!"

"Correct."

"Yep, and not some Mac Air thing wispy thing. Nope, I'm betting that you're more a MacBook Pro sort of guy."

"Good bet...right on the money," said Jerome.

Sam just roared his distinctive bellowing laugh.

"So, how'd you know that?" asked Jerome.

"First off you're left-handed. Saw how you adjusted your tie when you came in. Lefties are more creative by nature, according to neurobiology...they're right-brain dominant...more artistic, good with spacial relationships, and athletic."

"That's amazing."

"Besides which, I had a fifty-fifty chance of getting it right— actually a seventy-thirty chance...according to national sales numbers! HA-HA!"

After Sam gave Jerome his shiny new MacBook Pro—already set up and ready with two hard drives, one for Mac software and one for Windows, just to hedge Sam's bet—the two of them chatted. And they chatted. Sam knew a lot about a lot of things... he wasn't just a Renaissance man; the guy knew history, Shakespeare, Monty Python, vintage old movies, cars, and even plants. What's more, Sam had the greatest smile and loudest laugh Jerome had ever heard. And he laughed at just about everything.

"You're one of the happiest guys I think I've ever met, Sam."

"Well, thanks, HA! Never really thought about that. But yep....guilty as charged. HA! Got a good job, a great girlfriend, and people like you, Jerome. Life is very good."

Later that day, Jerome would learn from Paul that Sam had survived a particularly nasty case of colon cancer when he was forty—about five years ago; that he worked a second job to help pay for his mother's post-stroke care; and alternated evening and overnight care for his mother with his sister. He hadn't married his lifelong sweetheart because he didn't want her to assume any of his burdens. Despite all he was carrying on his shoulders, Sam acted like his life was one great cartoon full of adventure, fun, and unending curiosity and discovery.

Chapter 4: The Narcissist

One day during Jerome's second week on the job, Rachel was waiting for him. She had her "gottcha look" on her face. "What time is it, Jerome?"

Jerome looked at the clock and said, "9:15," as he walked to his desk.

"And what are your hours?"

"Look…"

"Your hours, please?"

"Nine to five."

"Correct…don't be late again," she said, pivoting smugly and returning to her cave of an office.

Later that morning, Rachel stomped out of her office with a piece of paper in her hand and pushed it toward Jerome. "What's this?" she said with a sharp edge to her voice.

Jerome took the paper, inspected it and said, "A press release that I wrote on Friday."

"And who approved this for release?"

"Paul."

"So, now Paul's your boss, not me."

"You were at a doctor's appointment, you recall."

"Which I returned from at 5:30….long after you were gone, I'm sure!"

"You actually wanted me to get your approval on a routine press release?"

"Correct," she said, crumpling it into a ball and tossing it on his desk.

It was all Jerome could do to refrain from throwing it right back at her with a few choice descriptors about her personality.

But he thought better and instead threw the crumpled release into the trash. Thus went a typical day for Jerome trying to work with Rachel.

Later that day, Jerome had his scheduled meeting with J.C. Just seeing Jerome walk by her office made Rachel chafe at Paul's special treatment of him — the coaching, all this do-gooder stuff. All while she had a marketing and communications operation to keep moving — everything was all on her head, she thought, but here was Jerome getting all this extra support.

When Jerome walked into the Starbucks, he saw J.C. sipping a coffee and reading the *Washington Post* on his iPad.

"Hey," Jerome said.

"Hey back at you. How's it going?"

That was when Jerome described how the morning — and just about every day, in fact — had gone with Rachel: her incessant badgering, controlling, anger, and seething frustration over Jerome's presence in the office, despite Jerome's best efforts to develop a positive relationship with her.

After asking a number of questions that Jerome answered in some depth, J.C. paused and asked, "Would it help if we discussed, even brainstormed, about how to deal with Rachel?"

"Yeah sure, but I'd be interested in any observations you have. I know you've worked with Paul and the company for some time."

"So, you'd like my perspective on Rachel?"

"That'd be useful."

J.C. explained that based on his observations and study, everyone has an ego — who we think we are. And that we try to protect that image of ourselves, by how we talk, dress, the cars we drive, our houses, and all the stuff we surround ourselves with. In a way, we draw a picture of ourselves to present to the world. We begin to fall in love with our image. "We're all narcissists — in love with our own image. With some people, that issue is stronger than others," he explained. "I actually call it the Wizard of Oz Syndrome."

"Huh?"

J.C. recounted how when Dorothy, the Tin Man, the Lion, and the Scarecrow finally reached to Oz and found the Wizard, he was just a little old man behind a curtain, pulling strings to make himself look all-powerful. In modern parlance one would call him a narcissist—someone who would go to great lengths to protect his self-image.

"Like Rachel," said Jerome.

"I'd say, at least to a degree. I'm no psychologist, and we're not on solid ground trying to diagnose anyone, but you might just be observant about when and how she tends to flare up."

"She's a control freak...in my mind."

J.C. explained that the control might just be her way of trying to keep her life from spinning out of orbit. "It's like you control what you can and sometimes that's like arranging the chairs on the Titanic. You can't control the sinking of the ship but you can control the deck chairs!"

"Wow, what a wild image!" Jerome said, laughing.

"Actually, if you recall the movie, they were actually playing chamber music as the ship sank!"

"So how does this help me deal with her?"

And in the blink of an eye, J.C. switched back into coaching: "What do you think it could mean?"

"Maybe she's not as secure as she wants me to think...maybe my presence is a big problem for her. A threat, of sorts."

"So, how do you think that threat affects your relationship?"

The two of them discussed some tactics in dealing with Rachel. Let her be right, tell her she's smart when she does something smart—help her hold up the image.

"Don't lie but use every opportunity to get her to like me. Maybe even trust me?"

"Sounds like a plan."

"Hmmm. That simple?"

"Not exactly, but it's a start. So, is that what you want to be held responsible for until we meet in a couple of weeks?"

"Yep. I'll work on my Wizard-of-Oz approach!"

When Jerome returned, there was an 8 x 10 piece of paper on his desk with a huge, scrawled message—See Me, ASAP!! —in Rachel's handwriting. *Here we go, he* thought. *What now!*

When he entered Rachel's office, she was on the phone with the budget people, saying, "That's ridiculous. I never authorized such an absurd expense." She paused as someone on the other end apparently said something Rachel didn't like. At that point she got red and slammed down the phone.

When she saw Jerome, she pointed at the chair in front of her desk and said, "Sit!"

She waved around an invoice from J.C.. "We're paying that J.C. Williams, that academic nerd, $1,500 bucks a month—out of MY budget—to coach a homeless guy!"

Jerome felt the blood rush to his cheeks, which felt suddenly very warm. He wanted to reach across the desk and shake some sense into her head, but of course, he knew better.

"Well, who authorized this stupid investment? Who?"

"I guess Paul did?"

"You guess, my eye! YOU and Paul set this up. You want my job—that's it, isn't it!"

"What?"

"I see it all now…you and Paul. Well, I'm an equity partner in this firm with some say on what happens around here. And, if I have anything to say…I…." she stopped short. She was on her feet, red as a beet, stomping out of her office toward Paul's office with the invoice in hand. *This should be a real show*, thought Jerome.

About an hour later, Paul's secretary Janet came into the office and quietly picked up Rachel's laptop, put it in her carrying case, got Rachel's purse, and returned toward her office.

Jerome just sat at his desk, trying to work at a project he'd been assigned that had a deadline well into next week.

About twenty minutes later, Paul called Jerome to his office. Paul looked upset, though he was trying to settle down by sipping some water. He motioned Jerome to take a seat.

"I just sent Rachel home for the rest of the week," he said.

"OK."

"She was beyond rational and began to say things that were rude, disrespectful, and way out of bounds. You'll be acting in her place. I don't want her calling in, texting in, or sending emails. I told her to get some help with her anger."

"OK."

"You're not the first outside hire she's had this response to."

"OK."

"Let me know if you need anything to keep things afloat. I need some time to digest all this," said Paul.

"OK." And Jerome rose to leave.

Chapter 5: The Pillars

The rest of the week was weird. Without Rachel there for three days, Jerome could actually just concentrate on his assignments, without all the drama. In fact, Paul had asked Jerome to work on Paul's acceptance speech as the Chairman of the Community Foundation at the annual gala. Normally, Rachel wrote all of Paul's speeches, especially something as important to Paul as this gathering — where he'd be in front of about 1,000 community and business leaders in tuxedos and gowns. By Thursday Jerome had started to do research, called the executive director of the Foundation for samples of previous year's Chairman's speeches, read a dozen of Paul's previous speeches, and begun an outline of the speech.

That afternoon, he and Sam went to lunch, as had started to become their custom. They usually just walked across the street to the local Starbucks for a coffee and sandwich. In the midst of their lunch, Jerome asked Sam, "How'd you become such a happy guy?"

That question took Sam aback. "Happy…hmm. I think I'm just naturally content with my life. I like the people I work with, my job, and my friends."

"Interesting. And I know you read a lot," Jerome said. "Anything you could share with me about what you've learned?"

Stroking his dark curly beard, Sam said, "Well, I have done some reading on the subject." This was his code for saying that he'd studied the heck out of the topic.

"So, what have you learned?"

That was like giving a professor a white board and a marking pen, or showing a dog a fire hydrant on a walk — both were irresistible!

Sam lifted his head from his coffee and said, "OK. I'll tell you about my Three Pillars Theory of Positivity." With that he pulled a beige recycled Starbuck's napkin close to him and pulled out his signature medium point, Paper Mate felt tip pen.

"I'm all ears, man."

"There's a lot out there. Guys like Dr. Martin Seligman at the University of Pennsylvania, Barbara Frederickson at UNC, Ed Dienner, Sonja Lyubomirsky…the list goes on." He jotted down the names as he spoke.

With that, Sam held forth. He mentioned that he'd spent a whole year studying the topic of positivity and happiness to develop his Three Pillars Theory. To illustrate his theory, Sam drew a rotunda-like roof and then three pillars to support it.

"I know this looks very Jeffersonian…rotunda and all that… but after all I'm a true University of Virginia alum. And we have to evoke the name of Jefferson at least once in every serious conversation!" Sam said with his loud signature "HA-HA-HA" laugh that always got heads turning in any restaurant or Starbucks. Sam knew how to laugh — loudly!

"OK…the three pillars that I got from reading all the stuff I could get my hands on boiled down to three BIG ideas."

He printed on the paper napkin three sets of words, in block letters, along each pillar:

GET SOCIAL—GET STRONG—GET POSITIVE.

Then he stopped and made several other notes toward the bottom of the sheet:

50-10-40 | Open System | WiFi | Fear—30 vs 180 | Engagement 30%/20%

Finally he looked at Jerome and said, "OK…remember you asked!" And with that Sam explained the research indicating that 50% of the variance for our set point for happiness is inherited from Mom and Dad, but that's all. Also, all that happens in our lives—good or bad or big or small—accounts for only 10% of our happiness. That's it. However, 40% of our happiness is under our direct control. We literally decide a lot about whether we'll be happy or not.

"Only 10% from all that happens to us in life?" Jerome asked.

"Yep, no matter if you get injured in wartime, get divorced, have a terrible accident, or win the lottery or the Nobel Prize…it drops or raises your happiness level only 10%."

"So that means I can't blame all my woes on my mother, father, or wife," Jerome said with a smile.

"Afraid not, partner—only that you inherited 50% of it from your parents."

Next, Sam pointed to "Open System" and "WiFi" on his paper napkin. Then he explained that the brain is an open system… unlike any other system in the body, such as the circulatory, pulmonary, or skeletal systems. And inside the brain there was an alarm system…called the amygdala…that was always on and warned us of threats. It creates the fight, flight, or freeze response when we are threatened. Leaders carry around a kind of "hot spot" WiFi system that communicates their mood (happy, sad, or mad) to those around them, especially direct reports…who quickly pick up the boss' mood—through the WiFi.

"When people sense the boss is in a bad mood, their attention gets focused on whatever threat she poses. In fact, vision goes from a relaxed 180 degrees of peripheral vision to as little as 30 degrees. That's why we make such poor long-term decisions under stress."

"Really....wow...30 degrees."

"Wait, there's more...as the TV advertisements say!" Sam said with a big HA-HA!

Jerome, too, laughed. "Oh, please, tell me more!"

Sam explained that engaged and happy people produced up to 30% more at their jobs. But only 20% were engaged. That means that 80% were under-producing by 30% with a total impact of a 24% "unhappy and unproductive" deficit.

"If your company is a $10 million company — then $2.4 million is drained away by a lack of engagement. A $100 million company — then you're dropping $24 million!"

"Holy cow!"

"Yep...this is a huge issue for people and businesses," Sam said, as he positioned his pen on the first pillar — Get Social.

Sam explained that family and friends were the innermost core circles of happiness. In fact, positive relations with those two groups were vital to having a stable, happy life. Sam then wrote down on his napkin the ratio 3:1 and explained that if you want a strong, positive relationship with anyone, you needed to have three positive interactions to any one negative interaction. And if you were married, you needed to have a 5:1 (positive-to-negative) ratio.

"Maybe that explains why I'm almost divorced!" Jerome said with a nervous chuckle.

"Same goes at work. But there you need a 360-approach," Sam noted on his napkin. Then he explained that it wasn't good just to use the 3:1 at home, but at work as well. And to be positive not only to your boss, but also to your peers and direct reports.

"Some people are great at kissing up to the boss, but they often suck at kissing down or across," Sam said.

"That would be Rachel."

"BINGO, my friend!"

Sam explained that research on success and happiness at work showed that these two qualities can be enhanced or threatened by the presence or lack of 360 support. Any group—direct reports, bosses, or peers—can help you succeed fast or help you fail even faster.

"No doubt, my friend. I've watched this play out. And right now I'm pushing a rock up a hill with Rachel."

"Yes, and you better figure out how to put some sugar on that rock, or you'll be eating a lot of gravel!" HA! HA!

Chapter 6: The Speech

When Jerome arrived at work on Monday, Rachel was already there working—head down—as if nothing had happened. The situation was awkward for Jerome, but he was interested in what Rachel thought of his speech. He'd sent her the speech by email along with an attached note saying that Paul had asked him to work on it. Jerome simply wanted Rachel's input before sending it up to Paul.

After a couple of hours went by, Jerome wandered up by Rachel's office and poked his head in. "Hey, Rachel how are you?"

"Fine," she said looking over her reading glasses like a professor who'd been disrupted by a student who decided to drop in after office hours.

"Did you get a chance to look over the speech I wrote for Paul"

"I did."

"What do you want me to do from here on it?"

"Nothing. I sent it along to Paul."

"Great…thanks. Can you send me the final that you sent forward?"

"When I get a chance."

"OK, thanks."

Nothing was forthcoming that day. Rachel stayed in her office most of the day, head down and serious.

Later, Jerome caught late afternoon coffee at Starbucks with Sam. "OK, Sam, how about lesson two of the "three pillars"?

"O yeah, of course, the second pillar. He pulled over a fresh paper napkin and wrote on the top of it:

The Second Pillar—Get Strong at Work

Then he added the following words to the napkin:

Know Yourself (360/MBTI/Strengths) | Work in strengths or Work-in your strengths| Calling, not a job | Teams—diversity, match strengths, champion, set challenging goals, think BIG.

"OK...this part is simple but complex." He explained that to make progress toward a happy, positive life, you had to first know about yourself....your likes and dislikes, strengths and weaknesses. There are plenty of instruments out there that can help anyone figure out what makes them tick. First, the idea of a 360 assessment made a lot of sense to find out what people who work with you think about how you "show up."

Then Sam took a big sip of coffee before saying more. "This instrument—and there are any number of them available—provides you with a reality check from the people who are around you every day," he said. "The MBTI and StrengthsFinder were also good instruments for pointing out your abilities—a useful guide to use with coworkers and team members. I'd say these instruments might be especially helpful with husbands and wives!" Sam winked.

"No doubt I could have used them a while ago," Jerome said.

"Better late than never."

Sam then explained that working in your areas of strength most of your day makes you happy.

"What if your job makes you have to work in areas you're not great at?" Jerome asked.

"Then you 'work-in' your strengths. Maybe you take on an extra assignment or you volunteer—like if you love to coach, maybe volunteer to coach a youth sports team."

"Work in or work-in your strengths," Jerome mused out loud.

"Exactly!" Sam replied, holding his cup of coffee as if he were offering a toast.

At about that moment, Jerome got a text from Paul: "Stop by my office at five before you leave tonight…about the speech."

"Well, I better get back. So, 'to be continued' with my happiness lessons."

Sam smiled and nodded as they both got up and headed back to the office.

When Jerome came into Paul's office, he saw Rachel seated there as well.

Paul was holding a print-out of the speech in his hands and did not look happy. "Jerome, last week I asked you to work on this speech. And I expected to see a draft Friday, but just got it today."

"Yes, I wanted Rachel to look it over and add to it."

"OK…but the speech I got today had Rachel's name on it as principal speechwriter for this speech. Is this true or not?"

At that moment, Rachel looked up at Jerome with a look that was not angry, but pathetic — more of a plea for him not to rat her out.

Jerome looked at her and Paul and then said, "Look whatever comes out of the office is Rachel's responsibility. Whose name is on the speech is irrelevant to me. And I'm more than sure she had any number of excellent edits to make it a good speech."

"Oh, it's an excellent speech, no doubt. I'm just wondering about where the credit goes."

"I'd say it goes to our unit. It's a team thing."

Rachel shot Jerome a-thank-you glance but stayed mute.

"OK, I get that — a team thing. I like that. OK."

When they go back to their offices, Rachel stopped by Jerome's desk. "Look, I appreciate what you did in there with Paul. You…"

"You're welcome." He paused and then said, "I also need you to know how I want to be treated going forward."

He explained to her that she was the boss. And, that things were going along well before he came along.

"All I want you to do is to respect me, like I respect you. We're a team. If you can do that, I'm behind you in every way possible. But if not...I'm out of here and will let Paul know exactly why. "

At that moment, he watched her upper body stiffen up and sharpen her gaze turn into a stare, approaching a glare.

"Before you react or respond, please, I ask you to take some time to digest what I just said. It's not a demand, I'm not being insubordinate, just outlining my conditions for staying here," Jerome said, standing up and towering over her. Then he paused for a moment and said, "I need to get to a meeting. Maybe we can chat later." And with that, he left.

Rachel was too stunned to talk—which was not exactly her default mode.

Jerome made himself scarce for much of the next day, finding excuses to be places other than wherever Rachel was. At the end of the day, Rachel was in the office alone. It was a quiet time of the day when most folks had left. Jerome thought he might test the waters by poking his head in and saying good night.

"See you tomorrow," he said. He could tell he'd almost startled her from the heads-down task she was involved in.

"Wait a minute. I want to talk to you."

"OK."

When he sat down, she began, "I've been thinking about what you said and it sounded like a threat to me."

Jerome remained silent.

"Was it?"

"No."

"Then what was it?"

"An appeal for respect. You respect me, I'll do the same for you. Simple as that."

"How do I know you won't get your 'feelings' hurt?" She put "air quotes" around *feeling*. "How do I know you won't then go running to Paul about it?"

"Because I will never say anything to Paul that you won't hear first. If I have a beef with you, I'm coming right to you first. Period."

"Hmm. Really."

"Really."

She seemed to mull this over, without appearing to be completely convinced.

"And if you don't....I will," Rachel said.

Jerome put his hand up like a cop stopping traffic. "Please stop there, Rachel, because it sounds like you're about to threaten me, and I just do not want go there. I don't threaten you, you don't threaten me."

Rachel actually reeled back in her chair, thinking to herself *Who the hell is this new guy?*

Jerome cleared his throat. "How about we agree on going forward respecting each other as colleagues and take if from there?"

Rachel was doing a lot of internal calculation and assessment. Her instinct told her that for now, at least, it was best for her to give it a try.

"OK."

"Thanks," Jerome said, standing up. "See you tomorrow."

"OK, yeah."

Chapter 7: The Dinner

Jerome arrived at the restaurant about fifteen minutes early to get a good table, something in the back where he and Sarah could talk. He had scoured the Goodwill store for the best "new" suit coat he could find. It was a blue blazer that looked brand new — a Brooks Brothers. He wore a blue and white striped shirt and gray pants that were a bit more worn than the jacket, but still crisp looking. He'd taken everything to the cleaners and had it all pressed and starched. He'd gotten a haircut and his beard was trimmed. Tall and slim, he wore the clothes with dignity and style.

Sarah arrived wearing a gray suit and looked as if she might have come directly from work. When he spotted her at the hostess station, he held up his hand to attract her attention. She picked up his wave, nodded and came his way. As she approached, he thought about what a great-looking woman she was. Tall, lean, and perfectly adorned in every way. When she got closer, Jerome rose from his set to greet her.

He stepped forward and tried to give her a hug, but could feel her reserve and backed off. "Hey, thanks for coming crosstown."

"That's fine," she said, and sat down.

Once they were both seated, Jerome noticed Sarah kind of staring at him. "Everything OK?"

"Yes, yeah sure. You look just as good as I've seen you look in a long while."

Jerome was always embarrassed by praise. He just smiled and said, "Thanks. And you look as wonderful as you have — as always."

"Thanks," she said, then stiffened as if to shake off the tit-for-tat session. "What's good to eat here?"

"Got me, my first time. Now, soup kitchens, I can tell you something about them!"

She laughed, flashing her great white teeth. It had been such a long time since he'd seen her laugh. Now he was also laughing. They were laughing together. Together, he thought.

They ordered their food and drink. She got a gin and tonic, but he stuck to tonic and a lime.

"So, we need to discuss the money Paul has offered in memory of Mary Alice," she said. And as soon as she said Mary Alice's name, her voice caught.

"Well, I guess first we have to agree to holding off the divorce by six months. I know I'm fine with that, but not sure that's something you want."

She looked at her drink and said, "Not really."

"OK then, let's just enjoy dinner, and we'll forget the whole deal."

They went back and forth, but eventually she agreed to at least not push the offer off the table. Once they agreed to just talk about the potential good the money could do teaching kids not to text and drive, the night went better. They bounced ideas back and forth about what organization would be best to develop a program, what the potential was to scale it nationally, and the complications that it might present.

By the end of the evening, she had asked him about his new job, and he regaled her with Rachel stories. And she told him about a few of her business dealings—leaving the both of them laughing.

"I wanted to ask you if maybe we could get together in a couple of weeks again?"

She hesitated and took a drink.

"Look, I'd understand if you said no. I just thought we had fun catching up...and..."

"You'd make a crappy negotiator, Jerome. You're already undercutting your own offer!"

He laughed.

"Let's just play things as they come."

"Sounds good!"

They got up and left the restaurant, and he walked her to her car, across the street. He stuck out his hand to shake and say goodnight, but this time, Sarah leaned in and gave him a hug and kiss on the cheek. On his way home, Jerome touched that cheek a few times.

That Monday at work, he met Sam for lunch at Starbucks and told him all about the date with his wife. Sam was genuinely happy for Jerome and grinned. After catching up on the date, they talked about Sam's weekend working on his YouTube video channel — he'd become quite the video producer — a tech channel for people with common home tech problems, like how to set up a router, how to troubleshoot problems, how to buy a laptop, and the like. He'd started the channel on YouTube on a lark, but it had started to attract thousands of hits a month, so he monetized it — put Google ads on the channel — and now he was making several hundreds dollars a month.

"Must make you feel good, Sam," Jerome said.

"Yes it does, and the money doesn't hurt either! HA-HA!"

"So," said Jerome, "I want to finish our discussion. You've told me about the first two pillars of happiness — Get Social with family and friends and Get Strong at work. What's left?"

"Glad you asked, " Sam said with a satisfied grin on his face. He pulled a paper napkin toward himself and pulled out his felt-tipped pen. Then , before speaking a word, he made these notes:

The Third Pillar: Get Positive in Your Activities

Physical — meditate, work out, diet and sleep | Psych — stop ruminating, start savoring, say yes and invest in positive activities. | Practice positivity…Gratitude, Kindness, Optimism/Hope and Love.

He looked up at Jerome. "You remember the movie Forest Gump, when Forest says, "Stupid is as stupid does!"

Jerome chuckled and nodded "yes."

"Well, same here. Positive is as Positive does! You want to be positive, you better practice it."

"Makes sense."

Sam explained that physically there were a number of things to do. Meditation—just slowly breathing in and out for ten to fifteen minutes a day can have a real effect on your body and mind. "The way I do it is to hold my breath for about thirty seconds and then the first breath you take is a deep belly breath. And that primes the cycle of breathing for me. Every time I meditate, things slow down and confusion clears. I use it often in the afternoons to slow down my day, which can get hectic."

"Great, thanks."

Sam then explained the obvious benefits of getting fit, but admitted that walking was about as rigorous as he got. But 150 minutes a week of good walking had a real impact. And when it came to diet, Sam confessed that eating was his challenge, but he was working on portion control and getting help from his friends.

Psychologically, Sam had learned NOT to ruminate about bad things that happen along the way. "Dwelling on why something happened keeps you from moving on. Better to learn from the event but to move on—and not spiral into a negative funk." He explained, on the other hand, when you have a good thing happen, think about it as often as you'd like, and you'll get a positive re-charge every time.

Then he told Jerome about John Gottman's research. "Dr. Gottman is a guy who studied happy marriages for more than thirty years. And when an editor of the *Harvard Business Review* interviewed Gottman, the editor asked him for the single best piece of advice for having a good relationship with a spouse.

Gottman thought and said that you should always say yes...as a way of starting out things. Yes, that's a great idea...let's try it. Yes, yes, yes!"

Jerome couldn't help interrupting. "Man, where was Gottman when my marriage was on the rocks! Damn. I said No, no, no. Could have been a poster child for proving his theory in the negative!"

"HA-HA," Sam bellowed, turning a few heads as was common whenever he roared.

Finally, Sam talked about "practicing positivity." There are about ten positive emotions that bring about a state change toward positivity. Some of the key ones are gratitude, kindness, optimism and hope, and love. He explained that by just keeping a daily list of three things you were happy for creates a strong sense of gratitude.

"When it comes to kindness, the research shows something interesting," Sam said.

"Like what?"

Sam explained that if you practiced five intentional kind acts on a specific day, over time, you became more positive. "I have what I call Kind Wednesdays. So on Tuesdays I make a list of who I'm going to be kind to and what I'll do on Wednesday. I've sent flowers to my doctor's receptionist, taken coffee over to the guys who work on my car, and sent short notes of thank you to friends and family. I often will set a goal to be nice to two people in traffic! Doesn't have to be anything major, just deliberate and regular."

Then, he finished up his lesson with a discussion of the power of optimism and hope. One way to "practice optimism" was to simply keep a journal for about four to five days, writing about your "ideal self." What would it look like if the next one to three years went exactly as you wanted them to go? Just writing out a description and then maybe some things you'd have to do to make that happen takes you down a very positive and direct path. It's like having a personal strategic plan.

"Great ideas, Sam. Just talking about them, I feel better."

"HA-HA!" Sam roared.

Chapter 8: The Transition

Saturday night, following his meeting with Sam about the Third Pillar of getting positive in your activities, Jerome decided to get to bed by ten at night, which had been rare for him. But he was determined to get on a "positive track," and he'd start by simply getting to bed at a decent hour.

When he awoke at six Sunday morning in his room at the local Goodwill, he put on a pair of Nike's and the running clothes that he'd bought on Saturday at the Goodwill store, the day after talking to Sam. It had been years since he'd laced up running shoes to take a run, and it felt weird until he hit the pavement. That's when it all came back, like riding a bike. One foot and then the other—first a walk, then he naturally broke into a trot. Pretty soon, he hit a rhythm. He was puffing more than he remembered when he had been running several years ago. Despite that, he felt good—very good.

When he got back, he ate scrambled eggs and toast and half a cup of coffee in the Goodwill cafeteria. After breakfast, he went back to his room. Sam had recommended that he get a small notebook and keep it in his medicine cabinet. Prior to brushing his teeth, he could use the notebook to write down three things that went well that day. He'd decided to do it at night, and tonight would be the first. He wrote down the following:

I'm grateful for:

1. Running in the morning.
2. I had a great egg today.
3. The sunrise this morning.

The next day, Monday, Jerome walked to work with a lighter spring in his step. It wasn't anything dramatic; he just felt good. As he walked, he even meditated on his boss Rachel. He pictured them having a good day together and what that image would look like, about how things would be better, and work would be more productive and fun. And, when he got to the office building, he was ready to take things on.

He settled into his desk, fired up his laptop, and found a cup of coffee, which he carried up to Rachel's office. "Hey, how are you?"

Rachel was deep into a document she was writing. "Huh?"

"Hope you had a great weekend."

"What?"

"Your weekend."

"Yeah. What's with you?"

"What?"

"You're like cheery or something."

"Nope, just feeling good. Brought you a cup of hot coffee."

"Sure. Yeah. OK. Thanks."

Jerome filled his week with a bunch of little experiments. On a card he'd written out *Gratitude, Kindness, Optimism and Hope, and Love.* Every day, he moved the card to different position to remind himself. Sam had mentioned that doing it for about a month would imprint the habit of focusing on the positive sign in his mind. And it was working. It reminded him to wish people a happy day, to say good morning and goodnight to Rachel. He complimented Janet, Paul's assistant, on her new dress. Helped Sam with a documentation project that was giving him a fit. Made it a point to hold open the door for people as often as he could. Tried to catch people doing good things, so he could complement them.

And mostly he started to see things though a brighter lens than ever before.

The list of positive things he did grew every day with simple acts of kindness and decency. It was so amazingly simple—and so powerful. At the same time, his Gratitude Notebook was being filled every night with simple daily blessings for which he was thankful. For example, one night he wrote:

I'm grateful for:

1. The sound of wind blowing in the trees
2. My new residence at Goodwill
3. Jack, a new resident

Another day's entry went like this:

I'm grateful for:

1. My job
2. Lunch with Sam
3. Rachel

The next week, he continued to practice positive activities. He started trying to meditate once a day in the afternoon for about fifteen minutes in the bathroom stall—he'd tried to find a place where he could get privacy and that was the best he could do for now at work! He continued his early morning running routine and even began to look forward to it as part of a regimen.

Then he decided to take on Sam's tip about kindness and designated Wednesdays as "Kind Wednesday." On Tuesday, he planned five intentional acts of kindness to be done every Wednesday. He remembered Sam telling him that they didn't have to be big, but had to be intentional. So, his first Kind Wednesday list included the following:

1. Send Paul a thank-you note for the job
2. Send Sam a thank-you email for all his help
3. Give a big tip to the coffee guy at Starbucks
4. Send flowers to Sarah
5. Help a stranger

And when he awoke on Wednesday, Jerome felt like he was embarking on a scavenger hunt. He had his list and he was ready.

First thing he did after his run was to write out a thank you note to Paul.

Paul,

> I just wanted to tell you how grateful I am for the opportunity you've given to me and also to Sarah. It's been a wake-up call for me, especially, and hard to put into words. Just know that I'm in your debt forever and hope to pay it forward in my life to others.

Many thanks,

Jerome

He put the note in an envelope and took it to work with him. And when he got there, dropped it off with Janet to give to Paul.

Next, he sent a short note to Sam, thanking him for all his help on happiness. He kept it brief because he'd see him later that afternoon either for lunch or coffee.

When he went to Starbucks for his morning coffee, he slipped a couple of dollars into the tip jar. Jerome was trying to do it anonymously — but the barista saw him and said, "Hey, thanks, man!"

Jerome just nodded and said, "Thanks for all you do."

Later that morning he ordered the flowers for Sarah. The woman on the phone asked, "What do you want the card to say?" Racing through his brain were words like — Love, fondly, thanks, hope. But finally he settled on simplicity — "Jerome" — then checked off #4 from his list.

The last action to take on was finding a stranger to help, and he found her when he got back to Goodwill. A young woman, maybe in her early thirties, wearing a worn army field jacket and scruffy jeans, stood outside the store. She looked as though life hadn't been good to her. She was riffling through her wallet as if she were counting how much she had. He remembered those days on the street when a dollar or two made such a big difference.

Jerome pulled out a $10 bill and crumpled it in his hand. Then he walked over toward the young woman. When he was about three feet from her, Jerome dropped the crumpled bill in his pocket on the ground.

Then he approached her and said, "Excuse me, miss." At first she didn't realize he was talking to her. "Miss, is that your money over there?" he said pointing to the crumpled bill that he'd dropped. She perked up and then walked toward it, unrolled it and said, "Oh, I guess, ah. Thank you," she paused and then looked at him again and said, "Thank you, sir."

"Happy to help."

Next, Jerome started to think about the idea of optimism — starting with his ideal self — that Sam had mentioned. It was weird trying to figure out what that really was, so he did some searching and found a book called *Wellbeing* written by Tom Wrath and Jim Harter from Gallup. The authors developed a theory after Gallup conducted research in 150 countries about what constituted well-being in people. The discovered five elements: Career Wellbeing, Social Wellbeing, Financial Wellbeing, Physical Wellbeing, and Community Wellbeing. So, Jerome thought he'd go with the five elements and write for twenty minutes in his black notebook about his Ideal Self in terms of the first element.

He started this way:

> Ideal Self: Career Wellbeing: Well, I've been on a professional hiatus, but things have gotten much better over the past couple of months. This new opportunity given to me by Paul has been amazing. Starting to kick off the rust on my writing skills. Getting back some creative juices numbed by the booze....

The writing went on for several pages, as Jerome described his ideal future self regarding his career:

> My Ideal Career in three years will have me writing creative stuff along with my professional

writing. I'd like to be writing more and more sophisticated executive level pieces. Maybe I could coauthor or ghost write an article for Paul or someone for a major magazine. I also see myself even considering starting my own company — maybe — my own PR shop. I'd find a neat office building with other creative types to hang around with and share ideas….

For the next four days, he wrote for twenty minutes, each day a different topic, following the remaining elements laid out in the Wrath and Harter book: Social Wellbeing, Financial Wellbeing, Physical Wellbeing, and Community Wellbeing. The writing at first amused him and then astounded him. When he allowed himself to dream about the future, things unfolded in unexpected ways. For example:

My Ideal State in 3 years--Social Wellbeing: I'll have several good friends to share my life with. We'll care about each other, be honest with each other, and help each other. At work, I'll have deeper roots. Be involved in the social fabric of the place. Maybe play on a team, hang out with people, get lunch with a wider group of folks. And, I'll get back with Sarah!

As he wrote that last sentence, it surprised him because he'd not even let such a thought enter his brain since their separation.

That was the precise moment that he began to think of love — an emotion he'd not engaged with for a very long time. This emotion would prove more difficult than the others because it had been the deepest buried. Love, he thought, and Sarah's face came to mind, as did Mary Alice's, sadly so.

One evening after a long week, when Jerome got to his room, he pulled out his black notebook and wrote down the following notes to remember what he had been practicing all week:

Jerome's Notebook

Pillar III: Get Positive in Your Activities

Get Fit Physically: Meditation, Physical Fitness, Diet, Sleep, Fit Teams

Get Psyched: 50-10-40; Decrease Negativity, Stop rumination, Savor good thoughts, Invest in positive activities, Just say YES, Cultivate positive habits

Practice the Big 4:

1. *Gratitude – Three Blessings Journal. Tell people. Teams – Positive Priming – express gratitude to them*

2. *Kindness – Kind Wednesday (or any day) –5 Intentional Acts of Kindness; Random Acts of Kindness. Teams – Celebrate Success, Kind Day*

3. *Optimism & Hope – Write about your ideal self 4 days in a row. Ideal health, Ideal relationship, Ideal job, Ideal family. Wellness (from Gallup – good place to start)*

4. *Love – find things in your life to love, cherish*

Chapter 9: The Beard

A couple of weeks went by, and Jerome had begun to feel more positive about his life. He actually felt like his default mindset was shifting, not all at once, but still shifting. Yes, he'd had some happy days and actually began to look forward to Kind Wednesdays — although he's really had to get creative with it. For example, he'd sent flowers to the Goodwill receptionist, bought coffee randomly for colleagues at work, and sent long-stemmed roses to Sarah. He'd sent emails to friends, handwritten thank-you notes to anyone who'd helped him, and slipped money into the hands of many "street people." And when it came to restaurants, the local waiters and waitresses loved to see him coming.

The one exercise that had caused him to change his mindset the most was the "three blessings" exercise he did every night before bed. Somehow the process of thinking back over his day, with a positive filter, made him realize just how many things had occurred for which he was grateful. Some days they were big deals, like when Rachel actually complimented him, or when Paul sent him a personal note about how much he appreciated something that Jerome had worked on. Other days, the items on the list were for simple pleasures like cold water on a hot day or a gorgeous moon at night or a relaxing walk to work. No matter how big or small, he was grateful for his restart and got more grateful every day. And that positive mindset seeped into his character, who he was becoming. It felt strange — in a good way.

One evening, while in the bathroom brushing his teeth and just before he writing his three blessings in his notebook, Jerome looked at his beard. First off, the beard had much more gray than it had a while ago. Then he remembered that he had stopped shaving the day Mary Alice died. In a way, it marked his descent into sorrow and profound sadness. The beard represented the beginning of the end to his marriage. It represented him quitting his job and drifting to the streets as a homeless man. In those short seconds all this flashed through his brain. He stroked the beard, looking at it from each angle in the mirror. That's when it came to him: Time to shave it off!

And shave it off he did, except for his moustache. Somehow, he could not get rid of all the hair all at once. In a way, it would have felt that he was burying Mary Alice—completely. He'd leave the mustache as a healthy reminder. Then he inspected himself in the mirror. *Not bad*, he thought to himself. He made a few faces to see what he looked like happy, sad, even mad with his new look. Then he got dressed and headed to work. By the time he actually arrived, he's forgotten he'd shaved. But he'd be reminded by everyone, all day.

The first to say something was Rachel. He poked his head in her office on his way to coffee, as he'd started to do routinely. And when she lifted her head up from her editing, she said, "Whoa, who are you?" He blushed and motioned like he was shaving. "You look totally different."

"Good or bad—different?"

"Just different. I'm trying to adjust."

"Me too," he said waving and heading toward the kitchen.

Later that day he and Rachel were discussing a new piece of collateral material they were writing and designing for the company. Rachel was dug deep into the details, but Jerome asked a couple of fundamental questions: "What are we trying to accomplish with this piece? Who exactly is the audience?" Rachel stopped what she was reading mid-sentence, looked up over her reading glasses, and said, "Exactly!"

Jerome just smiled.

"You do that all the time, Jerome," she said.

"What?"

"Get insights...sometimes simple, but still big. But I get lost in the details. Got to confess—I love details."

"That's just the way I'm built. Nothing special. You ever take the MBTI?" he asked.

"Yeah, Paul brought in a woman a few years ago who took the entire management team through it." She then explained that she was an Extravert, got her energy from people; Sensor, loved data and detail; Thinker, was logical; and Judger, liked to get things done.

Jerome explained that he was nearly her mirror opposite: an INFJ. Introverted, got his energy by being alone; iNtuitor, loved big ideas over small pieces of data; Feeler, makes his decisions considering the values, mores, and social conditions; and finally he too was a Judger, like her, and loved to get things done.

They spent the next twenty minutes discussing how they could divide up this project and maybe future ones so as to take advantage of each other's strengths. When they had wrung out this big distinction, Rachel said, "Terrific," and handed him the in-progress flyer that she was working on, "You work on this creative stuff!"

"No problem at all."

"Thank God."

The rest of the morning, Jerome literally hummed. He was in his element and the clock hands seemed to spin by. He was working hard but having a wonderful time. It wasn't work but almost play for him. When he looked up, he was surprised to see that it was already ten minutes to noon and he had scheduled a lunch with Sarah at a local restaurant to talk about the Mary Alice Foundation. On his way there, he thought of Sam's explanation about the difference between a job, a career, and a calling — that when you were doing something you loved, a calling, you were in a zone where time didn't seemed to matter. It was like when you read a good book and time seemed to be suspended. Today he had been in the zone of a calling, and it felt great.

When he walked into the restaurant, Sarah was seated reading a magazine. He quietly slid into the booth, startling her. She looked up at him and her initial look almost said, *And who are you, sir?* She said nothing as her mind surveyed his face. "Jerome? You shaved your beard. Wow, you look different!"

"Different good or different bad?"

"Just different. More like before," she said, her voice trailing off.

As he sat down, he touched her hand and this time she didn't draw away. It felt like a first date. He was nearly ready to explode with joy, and his smile gave it away.

"I haven't seen you smile like that for a long time."

"I've just found more reasons to smile," he said clearing his throat.

They had a great lunch, each telling stories about work. Jerome talked about how he and Rachel had slowly but surely become colleagues over the past five months, how they'd both discussed using their strengths to get the job done.

Sarah told him about some of her clients, in general terms, and some of the goings on at the firm. It was pleasant conversation. Then they got to the Foundation.

"Look," Jerome said, "I'm good with whatever you want to do with the money we'll get from Paul. "

Sarah explained that she'd like to build the account to start making it sustainable. She presented a plan that had both her and Jerome contributing to the pot as if he would get a real job. "I'm making some real assumptions here. What do you think?"

He hesitated and then said, "I'm sort of figuring out which way I'll go."

She leaned forward and said, "I don't want to rush you. I…"

He interrupted, "You're not rushing me at all. In fact, you've been incredibly patient. Paul promised me a chance for promotion at six months, and that's next month."

She nodded.

"Eventually, I'd love to have my own firm again."

"I'm good with that."

"But I'm not. I owe it to you, me, and Mary Alice to stabilize first. No new ventures for a year or two," he said. Then he explained that he planned to ask Paul for a full-time position and work with Rachel. He wanted to become financially solvent again. Repay debts he'd racked up before hitting the streets—debts that Sarah had paid off.

"You don't need to do that."

"Oh, but I do. So, I'm in on your plan and will contribute my share to build up the fund's endowment. "

Sarah's eyes began to well with tears as she dabbed the corners with her napkin. Jerome reached his hand across the table and squeezed her hand and she squeezed back. Then lunch came.

Jerome's Notebook

Pillar II: Get Strong at Work

~Know Your Strengths: 360s, MBTI, StrengthsFinder, DISC.....

~Work in Your Strengths or "Work-in" your Strengths: Capitalize on your strengths…and sharpen them by volunteering, taking on extra assignments, etc.

~Make Work a Calling: Job vs. Career vs. Calling

~Engage the Team—Celebrate diversity, match strengths, set goals, focus on something BIGGER.

Chapter 10: The Slip

The weekend before Jerome was to ask Paul for the full-time position at full salary, the bottom fell out. Saturday started like most. Jerome would usually get up and head to the local Caribou Coffee shop and get his medium half-caff cup of coffee and read the paper. It was the simple luxury that he allowed himself once a week. He read the paper from front to back—even stopped to look at some of the ads—and sipped his coffee for over an hour. For him it felt like taking a warm bath after a tiring workout.

As he turned the page of the *Washington Post* and moved to the Metro Section, his eye caught the date. September 30. He never even got to the year. His eyes locked onto that date, September 30—the exact one-year anniversary of Mary Alice's death. The sight of that date froze him. He could not move, even to turn the page. In his mind he could hear tires screeching, steel crumpling, and her voice screaming before it went silent. Right after the accident, he saw the scene over and over in his mind's eye until his psychiatrist told him to stop remembering it or it would drive him over the edge. So following his doctor's advice, he tried to summon up a large red STOP sign that he'd been taught to use to cease the "rumination," as the psychiatrist called it.

But today was different. For some reason he kept playing the scene over and over in his mind. And every time he did, he sank further into a funk. He wanted to pull out his cell phone and call Sarah to touch base, but he was ashamed and too sad to even dial the phone. If he had had a good friend or even a sponsor from AA, this would have been the time to call him. Instead Jerome just slipped below the water as if he were drowning in sorrow. Right there inside a quaint coffee shop on a clear, crisp fall morning, he fell off his recovery path and slipped into an abyss of sadness.

Nearly a half hour passed. Jerome was still on the same page of the paper—frozen in a block of darkness—the pain was unbearable.

He finally managed to stand up and walk out of Caribou into the daylight. The bright autumn light felt like fire. People were going about their business, some even laughing and smiling; dogs were being walked in the fall air. *How dare they! On today of all days, how could anyone be happy?*

That was when he spotted the local supermarket, where he knew they sold wine. For the longest moment he stopped and debated with himself about what he wanted to do. He remembered his last drinking binge, nearly six months ago, before he met Paul and before Sarah had come back into his life. He remembered that night on the street. It had been cold, which served as an easy excuse to slip into a bottle, like pulling a warm blanket over himself and his depression.

He stood outside the store like a statue. Then he went in and bought a bottle of wine — the first one he could get his hands around. He paid $6.69 for the chianti and walked — rushed — toward a local park that he'd haunted back during the days he was on the street. He unscrewed the cap and took his first drink. It had a sharper taste than he'd recalled. But by the fifth swallow it had mellowed, as had he. And when he finished the bottle, he tossed it and went back for another to take home.

The weekend was a train wreck. The more he drank, the deeper the pain, the more he drank. When Monday found its way into his head, he just rolled over and slept and drank some more. He ignored his cell phone all day. In fact, after the fourth call, he turned it off, so any call would go directly to voice mail. But it wasn't until Tuesday morning when he heard the banging at his door that he got up. It was Paul, with one of the trustees from the Goodwill. Paul thanked the trustee and walked into the small one-room residence.

"What the hell is going on, Jerome?"

"What?"

"You haven't shown up to work and you smell like a barroom. "

"I…no excuses. I'm. Mary Alice died a year ago. I…"

"Look. I know you're hurting, but Sarah, Rachel, and I have been worried sick about you. And you've been on a bender!"

Jerome just looked at his feet; he had one sock on and one off. He'd been sleeping in the same clothes he'd had on Saturday morning.

"OK, here's how this is going to play out, or I'm done with you. You listening?"

Jerome pulled his gaze from his bare foot to Paul's eyes. "Yes."

"You're going to take a shower and get cleaned up while I wait for you in the lobby. Then I'm driving you to a friend at Alcoholics Anonymous. And, you're getting into a program... today. If you don't, I'm done with you. We clear?"

"Clear."

That day Jerome attended his first AA meeting and met his sponsor, Ralph Rodgers, a banker who'd been on a similar ride as Jerome had been after Ralph's wife died of breast cancer. Ralph understood the rapid slip into the hole of depression. But he was a tough, no nonsense guy.

The weeks went by. It had been difficult, rife with temptation, and filled with calls to Ralph and even Paul. Turns out Paul himself had turned to AA when his son died, so he knew personally how tough this slip had been for Jerome. But he was firm. No sobriety, no job.

At work, Rachel had been supportive. Jerome saw a new side of her. It was as if she, too, had been down this road before. She treated him fairly and warmly both like an employee in trouble and like a friend. She pushed him and yet seemed to know exactly when to let up. For example, one day when she came into his office with copy he needed to revise, she found him paralyzed, looking out the window. It was late in the afternoon. She said, "Look, I'm dying for a cup of coffee. Let's go to Starbucks. I hate to drink alone!" That broke his spell. He smiled and off they went.

Sam had also been a great support, like a brother. He and Jerome had some long lunchtime and late-afternoon discussions over coffee about Jerome's falling off the wagon, feeling so alone and abandoned. "Man, we are your family, for better or worse!" he said with his signature laugh.

"Thanks, man."

"Back at you!" said the burly bearded teddy bear who accepted Jerome — warts and all.

However, Sarah could not accept it at all. She had called Jerome just after he'd gotten his thirty-day sobriety chip to explain that she wished him well, but that she couldn't take anymore. They'd be friends — only if he stayed sober — but even then there was no getting back together, ever. That news was as devastating as it was expected.

That night he'd been tempted to chuck it all but thought better of it and called Ralph.

Chapter 11: The Lifeline

Jerome continued to simply put one foot in front of the other. He stayed mindful—in the present moment. No dredging up the past and getting sad or angry and not projecting the future and getting anxious. He'd always been a realist—or so he referred to himself. So now was a time to dig into the moment. He remembered the Serenity Prayer:

> *God grant me the serenity*
> *to accept the things I cannot change;*
> *courage to change the things I can;*
> *and wisdom to know the difference.*
>
> *Living one day at a time;*
> *enjoying one moment at a time;*
> *accepting hardships as the pathway to peace;*
> *taking, as He did, this sinful world*
> *as it is, not as I would have it;*
> *trusting that He will make all things right*
> *if I surrender to His Will;*
> *that I may be reasonably happy in this life*
> *and supremely happy with Him*
> *forever in the next.*
> *Amen.*

He'd gotten back into the groove at work and had started producing high quality output—speeches, collateral materials, the entire gamut of public relations material. Rachel was pleased; even Paul seemed to be over the "incident." The months peeled by. Then one night things got even better.

He was shopping in the Goodwill store. He needed some new pants and was rifling through the men's clothes when he happened to look and spot a very attractive, light-skinned African American woman with long flowing hair, full lips, and sunglasses who had just come into the store. He did a double take. She looked just like Angelina Jolie, he thought to himself. He recalled a scene with her in *Tomb Raider*. When she looked in his direction, he quickly looked away as if having been caught stealing cookies from the cookie jar.

"Angelina" walked over to the women's clothes, turned slightly away from Jerome, and took off her sunglasses. From where he stood, he could not see her face, only a faint profile. So, he maneuvered around to a different table close to the women's clothes for a better look, not noticing that he was near the pre-teen girls' underwear table!

Suddenly, she swung her head around, her long flowing hair getting tossed over her shoulder when at almost the exact moment, Jerome looked down, noticing where he was, blushing and then looking up directly at her.

He was stunned.

She was stunned.

"Jerome?"

"Marguerite?"

He quickly walked over to her. It was awkward because he'd never hugged her before when they were on the street together. But when she opened up her arms, he did the same.

"Wow, you look great!" Jerome said, "Really."

"You clean up pretty well, too!"

They just looked at each other for a few seconds and then broke their mutual grip. Jerome invited her to get some coffee and they went to a nearby local shop.

At her insistence, Jerome told her all that had happened since they'd lost contact on the street. The job, Paul, Rachel, and Sarah.

"You both must be happy," she commented. "Are you getting back together?"

Then he explained his "fall" and that Sarah and he remained friends but nothing more. Divorce was imminent.

"Sorry about that."

"So, how about you? What's your story?"

She explained that Janet, Paul's secretary, had struck up a friendship with Marguerite after meeting her regarding Jerome. Turns out that Janet had a sister who had been a battered wife—like Marguerite. After Jerome took the job and got a room at the Goodwill, Marguerite agreed to Janet's proposal to take a room at Mary's Place, a shelter for battered women, where Janet volunteered.

Marguerite paused. "I was a mess, but Janet stood by me." She went on to say how she'd gotten a job as a waitress at a local restaurant and had even looked into going back to school—just saying those words sent a chill up her spine.

"Wow, I'm so happy for you. What a wonderful place to be."

They talked for an hour and a half before she looked at her watch. "Oops, I have to meet Janet and then my group. So, I gotta get going."

"You want to get together next week?"

"Sure."

They exchanged numbers and she left. He watched as she crossed the street and turned the corner, then went out of sight.

The next day Sam and Jerome were having lunch when Sam reminded Jerome that "getting social" would be the key to his long-term recovery. "We need each other. Ultimately, man, we are our brother's keeper." As he spoke he pulled out a paper napkin and scribbled out some notes:

Pillar III: Get Social in Your Relationships

~Engage Your Family

-Losada's Line 3:1

-Gottman 5:1; 4 Horsemen of
Apocalypse(Criticism, Contempt, Defensiveness,
Stonewalling)

~Engage Your Friends

-Sounding Boards

-Engage Your Co-Workers

-Your Boss: Prime relationship--Goleman's Vertical Couple; Liking and Cialdini

-Your Peers: Share with them; Don't go it alone; Humility; Focus on "We"

-Direct Reports: Engaged employees 30% more productive…only 20% engaged!! Gallup Studies. Let them work in areas of strength.

Sam took advantage of the situation to talk again about how a researcher, Marcell Losada, had found out through studying business people that we need people to ground and support us. In our relationships, we need to have a 3:1 positive-to-negative interaction with people we want to maintain a relationship with… at work, home, and with friends.

"Yes, I remember that you mentioned that ratio before once. Remind me again. again.

"Yep, it's 3:1, and if you're married, it's a 5:1 ratio…positive-to-negative interactions!"

"Wow….I remember the numbers now!" Sam then re-explained the research of famed marriage researcher and psychologist John Gottmann, who discovered what he called the Four Horsemen of the Apocalypse — the downfall of a marriage: Criticism, Contempt, Defensiveness, and Stonewalling. He explained them each to Jerome, who seemed to nod in agreement and also that he'd been guilty of all four!

Sam told him about how vital friends, co-workers, and especially bosses were to your life and the extent of their influence on it. "They're like antibiotics are to your body. All the people who surround you protect you from the assaults of life."

Sam explained that outside of someone's family, the relationship with a boss was probably the most important relationship a person could have. When you have a good boss, someone you like, respect, and think cares about you — work is easy, fun, and productive. But when you don't trust your boss or think the boss cares, work is tough, unpleasant, and unproductive.

"Amen," said Jerome, "Amen."

"I remember reading a Gallup study that said the only 20% of the people at work were engaged and that those who were engaged produced 30% more. You start doing the math on lost productivity at work, and it's scary!"

"Really," said Jerome who was doing some calculations on a napkin. "So 80% of the people are under-producing by 30% — or an overall loss of 24%!"

"Yep."

"That's pretty amazing. It you take an even a small company of $10 million; they're leaving $2.4 million on the table."

"EXACTLY," Sam said looking at his watch. "and speaking of productivity, we should get back to work."

"Amen, brother."

Chapter 12: The New Start

After six months of sobriety and several months of dating Marguerite, Jerome felt as great as he ever had in his life. At times, he actually felt guilty for feeling so well, despite the memory of Mary Alice's death. Nonetheless, he was on top of his game and for the second time in his life, deeply in love. He and Marguerite still lived apart because both of their programs recommend going slowly. But they were making plans for a bigger commitment to each other.

Work had gone very well. In fact, he and Rachel had become more than boss-subordinate. Rather, they'd morphed into true colleagues, working together on one interesting project after another and with great success. They had fun, laughed, and began to share their personal lives.

Paul had come through with his promise of $100,000 to the foundation, so Jerome and Sarah accepted the money together, including a publicity photograph for the media that Rachel had insisted on not only to get some ink for the company but also to let people know about the foundation. Shortly after the donation, Paul had called Jerome into his office to offer him a full-time, full-salary position as deputy to Rachel. It felt like an early birthday present to Jerome. Interestingly, he asked for a week to think about the very generous offer.

Jerome had been sketching out an idea for his own company focused on providing a business to support companies with writing of all types: speeches, web content, press releases, etc. He didn't want to run a PR shop per se because he didn't like all the relationship building associated with media relations. Rather, he wanted to be the guy who wrote the stuff that corporate PR shops sent to their clients. He thought of himself as an elf in the back room making the toys, not Santa Claus delivering them.

So, a week later Jerome met with Paul and told him that he'd love to continue working directly with the company, with Paul, and especially with Rachel. Paul knew of their fondness for each other, which actually had saved Rachel's job when she turned around her often caustic behavior. Then Jerome pitched Paul on the idea of Paul's company becoming Jerome's first anchor client. He laid out a one-year, renewable contract that would be cheaper and ultimately more effective and efficient for both Paul and Jerome. And Jerome mentioned that he'd already spoken confidentially about this with Rachel, telling her what he wanted to do, and after some discussion she completely supported the idea.

After many questions, Paul agreed to the contract! Jerome could hardly contain himself. Truly, this had to be one of the high-water marks in his career. That day "Paul Langer Communications" was born. After he called Marguerite, he called Sarah to tell her the good news.

"I'm very happy for you, Jerome. You earned this one."

He teared up. His voice, when he responded, was a croak. "Thanks, Sarah, that means a lot."

The next few weeks went by in a flash and before he knew it Jerome was standing with about seventy-five people in a posh hotel conference room at his own "Going Away—but Staying Onboard" party!

Paul spoke first and said wonderful things about Jerome. He told about so many projects that he'd worked on over the last year including speeches, the company's web site, press notices, and more.

"When I think of Jerome, the word competent just pops up. But also, I think about caring as well," Paul said. "Jerome cares about other people and had become a friend to many folks in this room. That why we'll miss seeing him every day, but we're so happy he's staying in the family as one of our strategic partners."

Paul started clapping, directing his gaze and upraised hands toward Jerome, who slightly bowed his head in deference. "So without further ado, ladies and gentlemen, let me introduce Jerome Langer, CEO of Jerome Langer Communications!"

For a second, Jerome froze, waiting for this CEO he'd just mentioned. Then, of course, he moved to the podium.

And when he took the podium, he promised to be mercifully brief but needed to thank some people.

"First, I want to thank Paul for his courage in taking the risk of getting me off the streets, cleaning me up, and giving a job. I will never be able to repay you, never. But I plan to pay your most generous gift forward with others.

"Next, I want to thank my former wife, Sarah, for her extraordinary patience and leadership over the years. You all know that we went through the devastating loss of our daughter, Mary Alice. However, Sarah kept things going, even when I lost it. And she was there when I got back on track, then off track, then back on track! I guess you get the pattern here."

People laughed.

"Next, I want to thank Marguerite, who was with me during those very dark days and nights during the depths of my sadness and despair. We were cold together on those awful winter nights and hot in the summer together, rained on, rousted, and looked down on. But through it all Marguerite was always there, quietly supporting me in the worst of situations. Her resilience was and is incredible, especially in light of the difficult life she lived through. And now we're together, I hope for a very long time.

"Finally, I want to thank my great friend Sam," he said looking at Sam, who beamed at the mention of his name.

"Sam taught me about happiness and leading a positive life. As many of you know, most every day Sam and I got lunch and late afternoon coffee at Starbucks. I hate to calculate how much money we spent there! We probably bought their CEO a new swimming pool!"

"HA-HA-HA," Sam bellowed, as only he could.

"Thanks Sam! So, Sam taught me that there were Three Pillars of Positivity. First you had to have a strong and supportive network of family, friends, and coworkers. Second, you had to work all day at the stuff you love doing. Third, you have to actively practice positivity—Gratitude, Kindness, Optimism, and Love. I've spent this last year working at all three pillars, and folks, it's been the best time of my life!"

People cheered, led by, of course, Sam.

"Sam, we'll always be friends, so this isn't goodbye but a huge THANK YOU, my good friend. Thank you so much for the gift of positivity and happiness. I'll always be grateful for you." With that he walked over to Sam and gave him a hug, something the team had never seen him do before.

After he returned to the podium, Jerome said, "Thanks to you all for saving my life. I plan to use it to help others and pay it forward. "

The applause was deafening.

Works Cited

Achor, S. (2010). *The Happiness Advantage.* New York: Random House-Crown Business.

Baumrind, D. (1964). Some thoughts on ethics of research: After reading Milgram's "Behavioral Study of Obedience." *American Psychologist 19*(6), 421-3.

Boyatzis, R. E. & McKee, A. (2005). *Resonant Leadership.* Boston: Harvard Business Press.

Brooks, D. (2011). *The Social Animal.* New York: Random House Inc.

Buckingham, M. A. (2005). *First, Break All the Rules.* New York: Simon and Schuster/Pocket Books.

Cashman, K. (2008). *Leadership from the Inside Out.* San Fransciso: Berrett-Koehler.

Cialdini, R. (2009). *Influence.* New York: HarperCollins.

Coutu, D. (2007). Making relationships work: A conversation with psychologist John M. Gottman. *Harvard Business Review.*

Diener, E. S. (1999). Subjective well-being: Three decades of progress. *Psychological Bulletin,* 276-302.

Dunbar, R. (June 1992). Neocortex size as a constraint on group size in primates . *Journal of Human Evolution 22 (6),* 469–93.

Dweck, C. (2006). *Mindset.* New York: Ballantine Books.

Fredrickson, B. (2009). *Positivity.* New York: Three Rivers Press.

Fredrickson, B. (2013). *Love 2.0: How Our Supreme Emotion Affects Everything We Feel, Think, Do, and Become.* New York: Hudson Street Press.

Gladis, S. (2011). *The Trusted Leader.* Amherst, Mass.: HRD Press.

Gladis, S. (2012). *The Coach-Approach Leader.* Amherst, Mass.: HRD Press.

Gladwell, M. (2005). *Blink: the Power of Thinking Without Thinking.* New York: Little, Brown.

Goleman, D. (2007). *Daniel Goleman@Google.* Retrieved from Authors@Google: http://www.youtube.com/watch?v=-hoo_dI-OP8k

Goleman, D., Boyatzis, R., & McKee,A. (2004). *Primal Leadership.* Boston: Harvard Business Press.

Hanh, T. N. (1998). *The Heart of the Buddha's Teaching.* Berkeley, Calif.: Parallax Press.

Hull, R. (1971). *Psychological Types (The Collected Works of C. G. Jung, Vol. 6) (Bollingen Series XX) [Paperback].* Princeton, N.J.: Princeton University Press.

Kahneman, D. (2011). *Thinking, Fast and Slow.* New York: Farrar, Straus and Giroux.

Kirkman, M. (2012, July 1). Bend-don't-break leadership. Personal interview.

Lencioni, P. (2004). *Death by Meeting.* San Francisco: Jossey-Bass.

Lyubomirsky, S. (2008). *The How of Happiness.* New York: Penguin.

Mednick, S., & Ehrman, M.. (2006). *Take a Nap! Change Your Life* New York: Workman Publishing Company.

Rath, T., & Conchie, B. (2009). *Strengths-Based Leadership.* Washington, DC: Gallup Press.

Seligman, M. (2012). *Flourish.* New York: Free Press.

Shenk, J. W. (2009, June; February 3, 2012). What makes us happy? Retrieved from www.theatlantic.com: http://www.theatlantic.com/magazine/archive/2009/06/what-makes-us-happy/307439/

Sifferlin, A. (2012, March 28). Why prolonged sitting is bad for your health. Retrieved from Time: Health and Family: http://healthland.time.com/2012/03/28/standing-up-on-the-job-one-way-to-improve-your-health/

Snyder, C. R. (1994). *The Psychology of Hope.* New York: Simon and Schuster.

Vaillant, G. E. (2012). *Triumphs of Experience.* Boston: Harvard University Press.

Offerings by Steve Gladis

Motivational Speaking

Steve Gladis provides an inspiring, engaging, and energizing session. Engagement venues can include the following:

- Company meetings and off-sites
- Breakfast, lunch, or dinner keynotes
- Leadership off-sites and retreats

"Terrific speaker… entertaining and informative style. Time flew and I learned a lot."
– Bank of America participant

Leadership Development

- Workshop sessions tailored to meet the specific needs of your organization
- Workshop length can vary based on session objectives and agenda

"Excellent course; very dynamic instructor. I took away many new insights as well as practical tips." – U. S. Government Accountability Office Participant

Executive Coaching

Steve Gladis has coached many executives in both the corporate as well as public service/government sectors:

- CEOs
- C-level executives
- Executive teams

Other Books by Steve Gladis

The Coach-Approach Leader (HRD Press, 2012)
A leadership fable about an elderly businessman, Leon Bausch, who takes over a company and teaches the company about the coaching process as the ultimate leadership model. With the help of Leon's longtime friend, confidant, and vaunted executive coach, J.C. Williams, Leon teaches his executives how to help people solve their problems by asking them key questions and by determining the Issue, the Impact, the Ideal, and the Intention. This inspiring leadership story allows the reader to absorb the backbone-solid content of the coaching process by attaching it to a heartfelt story.

The Agile Leader (HRD Press, 2011)
A leadership fable, *The Agile Leader* is the story of a leader, Luke Hopkins, who leads a national sales team. As he starts making changes and drives his team to achieve corporate sales goals, he runs right into the conflict, resistive culture, and company politics that all leaders must navigate to be successful. A former standout college quarterback, Luke seeks out his old football coach, Coach Danforth (Coach D) only to find out that he's died. However, his daughter Allison was given the Coach's last "Playbook for Leaders." She and Luke strike up a strong friendship, and using the tenets Coach D. wrote about (and illustrated with diagrams), Luke learns timely lessons for navigating the complex world of corporate America. Any new or experienced leader reading this book will clearly recognize all the challenges that Luke faces as he tries to make a difference.

The Trusted Leader (HRD Press, 2010)
A leadership fable, *The Trusted Leader* is the story of a new young leader, Carlos Lopez, who gets promoted to supervise his peers. He gets conflicting advice from his boss about how to take charge, and it backfires. Confused, Carlos seeks out the best leader he's ever known, Coach Jack Dempsey. The two agree to meet regularly at a local restaurant to talk about leadership. The Coach teaches Carlos about how to lead, while Carlos and the

coach learn about each other's secret, sad, but ultimately formative pasts. Finally, the coach teaches Carlos about the Trust Triangle—the critical key to leadership.

The Transparent Leader (HRD Press, 2009)
Written as a business leadership fable, *The Transparent Leader* is the story of a smart emerging leader, Stephanie Marcus, as she navigates the challenging world of business. Fortunately, she meets Lou Donaldson, who acts as a friend, informal coach, and mentor as he guides Steph through the complicated business ecosystem in which she finds herself. Throughout the story, Steph learns about clear leadership communication. She adapts and changes and becomes a more transparent—clear and open—leader. At the same time, she learns Lou's personal story, which helps her fully appreciate his wisdom. An especially good read for women in leadership positions.

The Executive Coach in the Corporate Forest (HRD Press, 2008).
Foreword by Marshall Goldsmith, the world's leading executive coach.
A business fable, *The Executive Coach in the Corporate Forest* is the story of a young, gifted executive coach, J. C. Williams, and his coaching relationships with his rather varied and interesting business clients—all with their own challenges. The book offers some engaging stories, has believable characters with realistic problems, and illustrates the structure and content of the coaching process. The book is a quick read and was written to explain the coaching process to executives who didn't understand it.

The Journey of the Accidental Leader (HRD Press, 2008)
Written as a business fable, *The Journey of the Accidental Leader* is the story of a young man who, like so many people, gets thrust into a leadership position he neither wanted nor asked for. What he does and how he reacts makes the book both entertaining and informative. This book is based on the author's practical leadership experience as a Marine Corps officer in Vietnam.

Survival Writing for Business (HRD Press, 2005)
To write well, you need to keep it clear and concise. This book

shows how and is a no-nonsense, virtual lifeline to writing success.

The Manager's Pocket Guide to Public Presentations (HRD Press, 1999)
This book is an indispensable reference for managers and executives who find themselves in the unfamiliar and often frightening position of having to give a public presentation. It is a compendium of tips that will help any manager learn the survival tactics of public speaking. A simple, quick read, based on the accepted theory and practice of rhetoric, it is also a confidence builder that will help any manager begin to overcome anxiety over public speaking.

The Manager's Pocket Guide to Effective Writing (HRD Press, 1999)
Written communication is prevalent at most levels of business, but especially at the managerial level. Your writing may be grammatically and logically sound, but is it effective? Is it conveying your message with the concision and accuracy that makes you an effective communicator? Whether you're a manager in charge of a group of writers, or just a person interested in improving his or her writing skills, *The Manager's Pocket Guide to Effective Writing* uses easy, practical, how-to steps to help you write better and ultimately make a better impression on others.

WriteType: Personality Types and Writing Styles (HRD Press, 1994)
Based on individual personality styles, this book provides new strategies for the four basic types of writers: the correspondent, the technical writer, the creative writer, and the analytical writer. Each person fits one of these well-defined writing "types." Once readers learn their writing personality and follow the writing process suggested in the book, they find writing easier and less anxiety producing.

Contact Information:

E-mail: sgladis@stevegladis.com

Telephone: 703.424.3780

Location: The George Mason Enterprise Center
4031 University Dr., Suite 100, Fairfax, VA 22030

Visit the...

Website: www.stevegladisleadershippartners.com

Leadership Blog: Survival Leadership http://survivalleadership.blogspot.com

Twitter: @SteveGladis

About the Author, Steve Gladis, Ph.D.

 Steve Gladis serves as president and CEO of Steve Gladis Leadership Partners, a leadership development firm focused on helping leaders and their teams achieve both success and significance through executive coaching, leadership development, and motivational speaking. Clients include executives and teams from publicly-traded and private corporations, U.S. government agencies, associations, and nonprofits. At George Mason University, he teaches leadership and communication courses. Author of nineteen books on leadership and communication, Steve is a former member of the University of Virginia's faculty and served as an Associate Dean and the Director of the University's Northern Virginia Center. He is currently an executive coach, certified by the International Coach Federation, for the Darden Business School's Executive MBA program and also teaches courses in leadership coaching. A former FBI special agent and decorated U.S. Marine Corps officer, he is a committed civic and academic leader. Steve serves on the Executive Boards of both the Fairfax County Chamber of Commerce and The Community Foundation of Northern Virginia and is active in philanthropic activities in the Greater Metropolitan Washington, DC, area. His company donates a significant portion of its annual net profits back to the community.

Contact information:

E-mail: sgladis@stevegladis.com | Telephone: 703.424.3780 | Location: The George Mason Enterprise Center: 4031 University Dr. Fairfax, VA 22030.

Visit our blog   Follow us on **twitter**   View our videos on You**Tube**

Made in the USA
San Bernardino, CA
08 February 2017